Acting and Action in
Shakespearean Tragedy

# Acting and Action in Shakespearean Tragedy

*by Michael Goldman*

*Princeton University Press*
*Princeton, New Jersey*

Copyright © 1985 by Princeton University Press

Published by Princeton University Press, 41 William Street,
Princeton, New Jersey 08540
In the United Kingdom: Princeton University Press, Guildford, Surrey

All Rights Reserved

Publication of this book has been aided by The Whitney Darrow Fund of
Princeton University Press

Library of Congress Cataloging in Publication Data will be
found on the last printed page of this book

ISBN 0-691-06630-2

This book has been composed in Linotron Sabon and Galliard
Clothbound editions of Princeton University Press books
are printed on acid-free paper, and binding materials are
chosen for strength and durability

Printed in the United States of America by Princeton University Press
Princeton, New Jersey

*For Eleanor*

# Contents

Contents

# Acknowledgments

AN EARLY VERSION of the fourth chapter of this book was published in *On King Lear* (Princeton University Press, 1981), edited by Lawrence Danson. Portions of Chapter Five appeared, in different form, in *Focus on "Macbeth"* (Routledge and Kegan Paul, 1982), edited by John Russell Brown. A version of most of the final chapter, except for the conclusion, was published in *Shakespeare Survey* 34 (1981), edited by Stanley Wells. In Chapter One and again in Chapter Six, I have adapted a few sentences from an essay, "Acting Values and Shakespearean Meaning: Some Suggestions," published in *Shakespeare: Pattern of Excelling Nature* (University of Delaware Press, 1978), edited by David Bevington and Jay L. Halio. Grateful acknowledgment is made for permission to use this material. I wish also to thank the John Simon Guggenheim Memorial Foundation for a fellowship which helped immeasurably in the book's completion.

While pursuing this project, I have been fortunate enough to be invited to share my ideas about Shakespeare with colleagues at a number of colleges, universities, and other institutions. There is not enough space to record the many kindnesses I have received on these occasions and no words adequate to express the sum of my gratitude. For the warmth of their hospitality, both intellectual and social, for all they have given me of encouragement, knowledge, and illuminating advice, I would like to thank Bernard Beckerman, Ralph Berry, John Blanpied, Philip Brockbank, Marvin Carlson, Kent Cartwright, Ann Jennalie Cook, Alan Grob, Terence Hawkes, Jean Howard, Cyrus Hoy, Dennis Huston, Susan McCloskey, Scott McMillin, Alex Newell, Edward Pechter, Norman Rabkin,

Carol Rosen, Meredith Skura, Michael Warren, Stanley Wells, and John Wilders. Closer to home, for some particularly helpful points of advice and guidance, I am most grateful to Maurice Charney and Paul Zimet. It is a pleasure to record a special debt of gratitude to Jonas Barish, who read a draft of the book and offered extremely generous and centrally useful comments. My work is honored by his attention.

Much of the book took shape in teaching, and I would like to thank the graduate students I have been privileged to work with at Princeton, especially those with whom I read the tragedies in English 525. At Princeton University Press, I have enjoyed the extraordinary editorial counsel and support of Miriam Brokaw and Jerry Sherwood, who, as all who have worked with them know, represent the craft and art of publishing at its noblest and best. My splendidly responsible typist was Leo Charney.

Finally, I cannot begin to describe all that this book owes to my wife, Eleanor Bergstein. Every page of it has benefited from her loving and rigorous attention. She is my perfect editor, my dearest friend, my heart's delight, my greatest teacher.

*Princeton*                                                                    M. G.
*March, 1984*

Acting and Action in
Shakespearean Tragedy

# I. Introduction

ACTING AND ACTION—the two terms, obvious, vague, familiar, stand at the heart of the theatrical mystery. The novice playwright learns quickly that he needs two basic skills: the ability to write for actors and the ability to create action. Without these talents, no degree of genius in characterization, plot, or language will help him. Their importance being granted, however, it remains notoriously difficult to say how acting and action actually *work* in drama. I would like to suggest that we can go a long way toward understanding their operation if we think of them not as separate processes, but as intricately allied. Indeed, once we look carefully at the relation between acting and action, the vagueness and over-familiarity that attend the terms begin to drop away, and what comes into view is a strikingly detailed perspective on the playwright's art.

One must start by insisting on the significance of a fact so obvious that it is generally ignored: acting is the major source of any audience's experience of action. In the theater, our sense of action rises almost entirely from the performance of the actors. Whatever "action" may be, it is felt as something *playable*, an impulse thrusting out at us from what the actors do, moment by moment, an unbroken flow of energy carrying us forward in time. Moreover, as we shall soon see, an actor's performance, *qua* performance, may itself constitute an important part of the action of a play.

But the action we feel and see in watching a play is of many kinds, and it evokes many kinds of awareness. There is, first of all, our sense that a play itself, and each scene in it, has an action of its own, an informing drive, that basic through-impulse which moves us forward. Distinct from this are the various particular actions we see performed by the characters on stage. We usually connect these actions to actions in the outside world—again in a variety of ways. For instance, they may strike us as imitating the actions of "real life": a door is opened, a king is killed. We are also aware that the actions we are watching not only imitate the actions of real life but comment on them. They show us the *way* of certain life processes: ah, we say, these are the dynamics of infatuation; this is what it's like to plan a crime. Finally, theatrical action seems frequently to comment on human action in general—on the nature of action and the problems of acting in the world.

The playwright, then, makes action out of acting—or rather he makes many kinds of action and many references to action out of a particular kind of action that we call acting. I am interested in the many relations among these modes of action, all of which clearly flow into and out of each other, each having the power to affect and change our experience of the rest. Surely their interplay is likely to prove central to the effect of any drama, and this presents a valuable opportunity for criticism—to see how the different kinds of action are called together and made meaningful by dramatic texts. The essays in this book explore the possibilities of such a criticism. They are attempts to understand some of the ways in which acting and action are related in Shakespeare's major tragedies.

So far I have given only a schematic account of the relation. It will need to be described in greater detail before it can be wholly intelligible and before my emphasis on it can appear justified. In the rest of this introduction, I would like to explain more fully the basis for my approach, and then go on to indicate some critical procedures which seem to me to follow from it.

❧

Let me begin by looking more closely at the idea of action itself. "Action" is a large foggy abstraction, and large foggy abstractions generally arise to meet urgent mental needs. There is no doubt that we are remarkably attracted by experiences to which we can attach the name of action. At one time or another, most of us have wished for a feeling of action in our lives (rather than, say, a feeling of disconnected activity). We like to be engaged in action, to see it, to think about it, to believe that it exists. People say, "Hey man, where's the action?" or that someone is a "man of action," or that tragedy must be concerned with action of a certain magnitude, and in each case they feel they are handling something that matters. To philosophers, action may be an obscure and refractory concept, but our casual use of the term plainly reflects the liveliest, indeed the most personal, of interest.

Action, as a concept, attracts the mind because it allows us to imagine a firm link between the self and the real world. We cannot think of action without bridging the gap between what is inside a person and what is outside him. When we use terms like "man of action" we are raising the closely related question of significant action, a conception which suggests that, through the idea of action, we may think of important events as somehow connected to the person who sets them in motion—as belonging to him in some way. Action allows us to think of what happens around us not just as events but as deeds, and to think of our private selves as somehow issuing forth into the world and making a meaningful impact on it.

What I am trying to get at here is not an abstract formula about action, but the emotional strength of its appeal to us, the texture of its involvement, as an idea, with our lives. I can do this a little more clearly by following up a notion I have just mentioned—that when we think of an event as a deed, we conceive of it as in some sense belonging to its doer. I find it helpful to approach action through the feeling which underlies this notion—the emotional sensation of *having*, of personal possession. What a wonderful thing it is, to have! And on what flimsily supported faith the notion of having rests. Nevertheless, it moves us. The appeal, the pleasure and power of having controls men's lives and shapes their philosophical vocabularies. The whole notion of attributes, especially of moral attributes, rests on the assumption that being can be had. Aristotle's *Ethics* is based, as he perceived moral thought naturally to be based, on *hexis* or habit, that is on what man has.[1] The love of wisdom and imagination has always been based on the faith that somehow the world can be put inside one's head. For every child, as for the artist or philosopher, the tactics of self-assertion—charm, tantrums, mastery of language, saying no or saying yes—are ways of demonstrating something he has already discovered not to be true: that he really has the breast that feeds him. And the idea of action, too, both practical and theoretical, is based on the desire to have the world—that is, on the feeling that it should be possible for the self to grip what is outside it.

This is plain from the way formal philosophy deals with the question of action. The recurring philosophical problem about action is a problem about having. When is an event an action? When it bears upon it the mark of agency, when it is someone's. When are a series of doings a single action? When they are linked by an informing efficacity. Is a man of action someone who does this and that, stubs out a cigarette, catches a fish? No, he is someone who makes a change in the world, a change to which he bears a significant relation. The difficulty always lies in bridging the gap between self and world; action is problematical because it is felt to be the bridge. In the symposium of the British Aristotelian Society, "What Is Action?"[2] the issue which divides the participants is that of apprehending and defining the system of links between self and world that the idea of action is felt by all of them to imply. Is thought an action, or part of one? Is will? Is choice? Can the noun-copula syntax of formal logic do justice to the verbal quality of action? Is logical entailment a satisfactory model for the relation of doer and deed? And if we look at more recent examples, the work of Arthur Danto or J. L. Austin, say, or if we look back to Hegel, we find, for all their obvious differences, the same locus of difficulty. In every case it is clear that "action" hums with the ticklish relation of the self to the world and the self's hunger to be seen in that relation.

We need not lose ourselves in the philosophical niceties of

the question. The relevance of the philosophical issue to our own everyday use of "action" lies in its demonstration that the word stands for a connection, however problematical, that we wish to make, seem to need to make, in thinking about an important phase of our experience. Action is a notion that allows us to think of a person as having what he does. Action, says Aristotle in the *Poetics*, springs from thought and character, and for "character" he uses *hexis* again—habitual predisposition to action, which, like our word "habit," derives closely from the verb "to have." Character is a *hexis* or having because it points to the difficult nexus between the self and its acts. Character is the quality by which our being may be said to have its doing.

Similarly, the idea of *the* action of a play reflects a desire for having. We talk about works of art because we wish to make them ours, to bring them within the boundaries of the self, to possess them in some way. Since we experience a play as a series of events occurring in time, any attempt to possess it requires a conception, such as the idea of action, which links separate events into a directed unity. The idea of the unity of action in drama is a way of allowing the play itself to have what happens as it runs its course, that is, of allowing *us* to have it as a complete experience. We watch Hamlet addressing the Players and we feel, or hope to feel, a larger efficacity of which this scene and all its apparent digressions are a fulfilling part. We seek the efficacity among the events of the play, a thrust playing through them, a single life informing them as the thrust of a man's being may be felt among the things he has done, if he has done certain things. We possess the life of the work through this principle. It is the way we have what the play does.

Often, indeed, we fail to notice how much our effort at possessing the life of the play contributes to our sense of its action. Our action as audience, in grasping and interpreting how the play "acts," can be very different from any of the actions we are witnessing on stage. A great playwright will often play the action of the audience's mind off against the action of his characters. Hamlet, for example, stabs through the arras simply and decisively. But when he does so, our minds go spinning around as we try to fit this event, which derails so many purposes, into a coherent picture of the play—of where it has been going, where it will go now.

One reason we like this kind of possession of fictive action is that we cannot have it with respect to our own lives and doings. We know we do not have ourselves in so full and unified a way. We first become aware of self as part of an experience of deprivation, the discovery that we are not coextensive with the world. We learn that they lied to us when they told us we were everything. (One of the qualities that makes *King Lear* so poignant is that the old king goes through this shattering discovery of infancy as if for the first time.) Much as we want it to, the self can't repossess the world. We know we don't really have our acts in the way our language implies we can when it uses "action" to describe human character or the experience of literary and dramatic art. That is, we don't really experience our doing as having, the making of something we keep, a changing of the world that is the possession of a self.

Here, we must remember that the notion of having has to be stretched to accommodate the materials of human deeds or events. Our desire to possess may indeed underlie our feelings about action, but the possession we are talking about involves not an object we can put in our pocket but a steadily changing chain of happenings which we experience as possible contacts with life. The idea of action finally engages the mind, not in a sensation of ownership, but in a process of significant contact—the visiting of our inner life upon the world, the unfolding of great events from the depths of individual privacy, the issuing of self into deed. It is this kind of holding on to life we want from our actions but know we cannot have. The philosophical haggling over action reflects the impossibility of joining the self and its doing, just as the uses to which we put the word reflect its permanent attractiveness to the mind.

Joining
the self with the
physical world.
the self is temporal,
while the world is
permanent

I refer to this, not to lament the instability from which all our pleasures spring, but to insist on the problematic character of action—and the deep-seated human difficulties to which the problems point. These difficulties are important to the study of drama—because they are bound up with the essential texture of dramatic experience. Nowhere do we feel the attractiveness of action more vividly than in the theater. When an actor steps before us at the beginning of a play, he appeals to us, above all, by communicating a promise of action. What we feel at this point is, I think, a promise of movement, or rather the presence of a complex of movements, already begun, which promise to continue for a satisfying period. The movement is primarily mental or imaginative—a movement of the spirit, Francis Fergusson calls it[3]—but it seems to resonate with physical suggestion, for instance the suggestion of a thrust out from the performer toward us, as he "projects" the character he is playing. Our sense of multiple movements is a response to the basic energy of acting, to that displacement of self, that charge of aggression that comes from (1) playing a part, the provocative thrust of changing oneself into something other than oneself, and (2) the accompanying thrust of making this change available to an audience. This energy cannot be sustained except by another current of aggression, which comes from what the playwright has given the actors to do, a thrust forward in time which we hope will carry us along until the end of the play. It is this third current of aggression to which we normally give the name "dramatic action," but it is clear that all three movements affect us and give the performance momentum. In fact, it is somewhat misleading to talk of separate currents, because the first two—the actor's creation and projection of his role—depend on the dialogue and events of the script, the same materials that provide the third current. And the events and dialogue, in turn, are projected to us through the acting.

The point is that, in the presence of dramatic performance, we feel with particular strength and excitement a continued thrusting out of the self into the world. The actor who comes before us at the beginning of a play provides a basic model for the process of human action. His movement of self-projection, toward us and into a part, seems directed not only to particular actions, but toward the very gap between self and world which the idea of action seeks to leap. Indeed, the type of self to which we pay most attention in the theater—the "character" presented by the actor—could be said to have a unique ontological status. It is not the personal self of the actor, but the self he creates by acting. And in that creation the gap between self and deed seems curiously to vanish. A character in the theater, the created self, is identical with the actor's deed. It is a self we watch the actor making—or, rather, the self *is* the making. We may be aware that Antony had an historical existence, we may even entertain some guesses about his nature before he comes on stage, but the Antony we know in the theater is not a figure from the past. The man we are watching is alive now—his character takes shape in an actor's living body. The self we observe is the actor's action. "Antony" is what the actor is doing now and now and now. Again, the issue is not the correct philosophical description of a theatrical character in performance, but the way the phenomenon of acting engages our impulse to leap the gap between doer and deed, between self and world. In responding to the actor, we feel the pressure toward action, the pressure toward the leap, with heightened urgency.

It should be remembered that we share in the actor's performance through action of our own. Acting has a powerful kinesthetic appeal. As we sit in the theater, we follow the action by internally copying or re-enacting what we see. Here we are not only responding to what the *characters* do; we are also re-enacting the actions by which the actors possess and project their parts. (As we leave the theater we may find ourselves walking or talking like one of the characters—a clear sign of the inner mimesis that acting induces.) In watching a play, we internalize that actor-like thrust toward utterance of the self which is the ground of all action in drama. And if the play is good, we feel the thrust working with revealing pressure against the conditions which make a full utterance of the self upon the world impossible. In tragedy in particular, the thrusting and testing of the self are likely to be extreme.

By now it may be clearer why I feel that the relation between acting and action offers us new materials for insight into the playwright's art. In any dramatic performance, acting, dramatic action, action in the "real" world, and ideas about action will enjoy an intimate and potentially rich interdependency. Acting and dramatic action are indissolubly allied, and "action" is a mental construct which drama is uniquely suited to explore. By looking at the interplay between the performance a text requires and the kinds of action and the questions about action of which it makes us aware, we should be able to arrive at a better understanding of how the play operates, how and to what purpose it engages our imaginations. The connections involved are present in all drama; in Shakespeare they seem at times under particularly intense scrutiny. Indeed, in certain tragedies, some of the problems I have been describing take on a direct thematic importance. *Hamlet*, for example, is painfully and analytically concerned with the mechanisms by which action claims to link private experience to the world. *Coriolanus* raises troublesome questions about the relation of action to "character." But such thematic motifs are only a small part of the story. The challenge for the kind of criticism I am envisioning is to learn to follow the relations of acting and action as clues to the deep life of a great dramatic text. Since the relations in any play are multiple, many points of focus are possible—more, certainly, than can be explored in a single book—and in the essays in this volume I have chosen to concentrate on what I hope is a suggestive, though highly selective, variety of approaches and emphases. Certain basic methods recur frequently, however, and I should like to draw attention to a few of them here.

&

First and most important, it seems fair to say that when we use the word "action" in its normal critical sense to describe the experience of a play, we are in fact referring to three distinct types of action, all of which influence us, and which combine and complement each other at every moment, often in the most subtle ways. For this reason, they are ordinarily confused. Certainly, many difficulties of criticism arise from not distinguishing them. They are: the actions the characters perform; the action of the audience's mind in responding to and trying to possess the events it watches;[4] and finally the actions by which the actors create and sustain their roles. Most discussions of drama run the first two together and ignore the third.

For reasons of efficiency, it will be helpful from time to time to refer to these three kinds of action by short and noticeable names, so I propose to adapt, very freely, some terminology from Aristotle and refer to the action of the characters as *praxis*, that of the audience as *theoria*, and that of the actors as *poiesis*.[5] I adopt these terms, as I have said, for reasons of efficiency. I am not fond of inventing terminology. But here it seems helpful, and not only because it allows us to use single words in place of long phrases. The fact is, the conventional use of the word "action" has so blurred the distinction between kinds of action that phrases like "the action of the actors" or "the action of our minds in responding to the actions of the characters" are not only unwieldy but essentially illegible, certain to be passed over as merely variant expressions of an idea presumed to be familiar. Something more emphatic is required to defamiliarize the subject. I shall try to limit my use of the terms *praxis, poiesis,* and *theoria* to a minimum, but I think it will be seen that they are necessary, if only to insist that they stand for distinctions it is worth training our minds to make.

The subject of *poiesis* requires further discussion here, since the performance of the actor is too readily dismissed as incidental to the dramatic experience. Acting is the basic material of drama. A play, finally, is an event which takes place between actors and audience. Others, of course, have helped prepare the event. Indeed, great preparation—which as far as

I can judge has always required a great text—is necessary to make the event great. But the event itself consists of actors speaking and moving before an audience; no one else, no other source of information or impulse, is involved. Thus the process of acting in any play will be as much a part of the dramatic experience as the play's incidents or its verbal style. More accurately, incidents and style will be perceived through acting, just as the incidents and style of a novel or poem are perceived through its language. This should mean that there will always be a significant connection between the small figures of acting—the local, repeated patterns of process by which the actor keeps his projection of the character alive and interesting—and the larger action of the play, just as there is a connection between the brushstroke of a painter and the felt significance of his design.

Any theater audience is aware that it is watching, not real life but a performance, and, if the acting is good, it will be vividly and pleasurably aware of the performance itself. The actor's action is a process far different from mere mirroring or imitation, and, at least in great drama, its most important effects are carefully enabled and controlled by the playwright. The specific kind of mastery the actor displays, the feeling of skill manifested and difficulty overcome, will inevitably influence an audience's response.

A good playwright makes difficulties for his performers, but he also makes the effort to master the difficulties artistically rewarding. Each great Shakespearean role seems to have its defining set of acting problems and rewards, and these bear a very suggestive relation to the larger business of the play. The problems which confront the actor who plays Hamlet, for example, are very similar to those which confront the Prince in making sense of life at Elsinore. The actor has to keep shifting styles, masks, aims, modes of attack. The part presents him with problems not so much of execution as of interpretation, of transition, of expressive coherence—the problem of finding a way to make sense of the innumerable, highly various, separate bits of execution that constitute the role. The actor's *poiesis* here must solve a problem parallel to those wrestled with both by the characters (*praxis*) and the audience (*theoria*). Most of the characters in the play—and its audience—are constantly trying to make sense out of a remarkable tangle of events and deeds which are often contradictory or mysterious. The difficulty of making sense out of action, one's own action and other people's, is a central motif in the play, and it is embodied, engaged, and kept before us by the accomplishment of any actor who succeeds in finding and expressing an inner coherence adequate to the major role.

When Hamlet reminds the players that they must not get lost in the whirlwind of histrionic effects of which they are capable as professional actors, but must instead find a principle of control, a tempering smoothness, he is of course talking about his own problems as a character, especially in the stressful scenes he knows lie ahead, where his rapid emotional transitions will perplex the court, his mother, and at times the theater audience. But Hamlet is also reminding us of the whirlwind of histrionic bits that face the actor who plays Hamlet's part. The kind of poise the actor needs to hold the mirror up to nature in the role of Hamlet is an emblem, a type of histrionic objective correlative for the kind of difficult spiritual readiness under stress that Hamlet, the character, is struggling to achieve.

My analysis of *Hamlet* has no doubt been too brief to be entirely persuasive, but it is the method, the kind of consideration being raised, that I wish to emphasize. Note that the acting qualities most under pressure in *Hamlet* are not the same as those which are stretched and tested in other tragedies. Playing Lear, for example, the actor is faced with the problem of continually reaching new and well-discriminated levels of pain. The actor who plays Antony must convey an impression of magnetic nobility even while doing far from noble things. In each case, as the chapters on these plays will suggest, the performance quality emphasized becomes part of the poetry of the play, the acting part of the action.

I am not simply saying that the actor of King Lear shows

us pain in a play about pain, the actor of Othello jealousy, and so forth. What I mean is that the histrionic problems posed by a role and the techniques required to solve them— the sense of a particular challenge met and overcome—can become a kind of imagery, a major component of the play's meaning. I first broached this idea some years ago in a book called *Shakespeare and the Energies of Drama*,[6] but at that point I only knew how to deal with relatively broad features of the performance design—as in the discussion of *Hamlet* above. Now it seems to me that a more rigorous analysis is possible, and in the following chapters I look at the acting problems of a soliloquy from *Hamlet*, a syntactical pattern in *Coriolanus*, a type of recurrent gesture in *King Lear*, to suggest how the action of the performer in overcoming specific and local difficulties helps create and alter the larger action of the play.

Another aspect of *poiesis* with which I have tried to deal is the speaking of the play's language. I hope it is clear by now that my bias is neither anti-poetic nor anti-verbal. There can be no question that Shakespeare's text must be primary for us, but his text is a design for performance. Every word is meant as a performed word. Shakespeare's task as a poet has an added dimension of complexity; he is composing in acted language. This, of course, does not refer merely to the gestures which may accompany a speech. The speaking of the verse is itself an important action, of body and of mind, and it can have a controlling effect in the theater. Little has been done to analyze the performance of Shakespeare's language as part of a play's action, and in a number of the essays, particularly those on *Lear* and *Macbeth*, I have tried in a variety of ways to pursue this connection between verbal style and dramatic design.

Finally, I have chosen to write about these six plays because they offer an obvious coherence and focus. They are among Shakespeare's most familiar works, confined to one genre, all produced, remarkably, within less than a decade. As tragedies, each is profoundly colored by the acting of a single dominant role (or two, in the case of *Antony and Cleopatra*)—which makes a particularly inviting focus for the study of *poiesis*. I agree with Kenneth Muir that Shakespeare wrote not tragedy but tragedies, and I have sought the relation of acting and action within each play, rather than in some presumed tragical entity of which each is a representative. Still, it will be seen that certain connections emerge. At the end of the book, I have commented on some of them, and ventured to speculate briefly on what they tell us about Shakespearean tragedy and tragedy as a genre.

# II. "To Be or Not To Be" and the Spectrum of Action

I

How DOES an action begin? Where does it end? What makes it an action? I sit at my desk, leafing through the newspaper. Suddenly I turn aside from it and begin to scribble this sentence on a pad. I clip it to some notes on another sheet of paper, run my eyes over them, mutter to myself, write some more, read it aloud, type it up. The paragraph is finished. I have it printed. You read it. Where did my action begin and end? What is really teasing here is not the problem of dividing the writing process into smaller or larger units of composition. The writing of a book or a sentence, the serving of a ball in tennis, an act of murder, might well involve similar components. What is hard to understand is how the components are joined, how each contributes to the others, what keeps them going, and where the chain stops and starts—how, in what we intuitively wish to call a single action, different pieces of inner and outer activity somehow get aligned and fused. The writing begins somewhere inside me, but with what? An idea, a wish to write, a phrase that "occurs" to me, the physical routine of sharpening six pencils and sitting down to the desk, the reading of the newspaper, the need to be busy, a random stroke of the pen? And what do any of these bits of activity have to do with what happens when you read this sentence? What was I doing when I muttered? Was this part of the action, and if so how is it related to the other pieces?

It is not surprising that philosophers regard action of any magnitude as a very complex process. If we think of action as a movement from self to world, from inner life to outer impact, we see that any significant action involves numerous events, inner and outer, movements of desire and thought, of body and, perhaps, of voice, adjustments of self and objects and others, which mysteriously appear to fuse in a single arc of accomplishment. To consider action from this point of view is to become aware of just how remarkable and perplexing the fusion is, how far-flung and hard to delineate are the components.

*Hamlet*, of course, is very much concerned with the concept of action, but it has scarcely been appreciated how sensitive the play is to the particular questions I have just described. Repeatedly, *Hamlet* makes us aware of how difficult it is to understand the *structure* of action, especially to grasp how an action is—or fails to be—constituted out of many separate human activities. At the same time, it confronts us with our own metaphysical hunger for action, that problematic longing, discussed in my introduction, to see events in the world as the possession of a self, and thus to find in action a reassuring connection between self and world.

In this essay, I wish to focus on the way *Hamlet* explores the process by which action issues forth from inner life and engages the world. Shakespeare's analysis is so subtle and fast moving that it is difficult to catch it on the wing, to see it, as it were, *in* action, as part of an emotionally charged experience which suggests many delicate distinctions. To meet this problem, I would like to introduce a few terms which may prove helpful to the discussion by standing, in a kind of shorthand form, for various portions or features of the action process. Three of these terms have been proposed by the English philosopher J. L. Austin, who observes that philosophers often fail to distinguish among what he calls the stages, phases, and stretches of an action.[1] By *stages* he means the mental preparation that goes into the action—decision, planning, etc. *Phases* comprise the discrete physical doings that combine to make up an action of any size—the separate strokes of paint in the action of painting a wall. The *stretches* are the successions of effect, ultimately very remote, that any action may have. A political assassination in Serbia involves Europe in a war which leads to a revolution in Russia without which *Dr. Zhivago* would never have been written, etc. In the case of a revenge play, the stages would include the revenger's becoming aware of the crime and planning his revenge; the phases might include stalking the criminal and running him through with a poisoned blade; and the stretches might embrace the death of the revenger and the installation of a foreign ruler on the revenger's throne.

Clearly, I have not chosen the example of revenge by accident. Revenge, we should remember, is not only an action, but an action which carries a manifest weight of significance. It does not consist simply in killing someone—that is one phase of the action, but it is not enough. It consists in killing him for certain reasons in a certain way, and in a way that is plainly related to the reasons. We cannot imagine Hamlet plotting to have Claudius die in heroic combat with Fortinbras, nor would *Hamlet* be a revenge play if in the last act Hamlet killed Claudius because the king appeared at the fencing match in yellow stockings. Like a "complete" dramatic action, the revenger's doings must be unified. Like action in the philosophical sense, they must link self and world. Revenge requires conviction, thought, intricate planning, the overcoming of obstacles, an execution that bears a plain relation to the crime committed and the outrage felt. Revenge drama was a remarkable dramatic invention because any revenge play must involve its audience in a great felt arc that reaches from the disturbance at the heart of the revenger to the killing of his enemy, an arc which parallels the arc of dramatic utterance whereby the unspeakable feeling in the revenger's heart becomes passionate speech on stage. Revenge drama allowed powerful feeling to utter itself not only in words, but in intricate, unified plot.[2]

Even this brief account of revenge, however, suggests some aspects of its action which Austin's terms do not fully control. When the revenger cries out in horror, for instance, is this an initial stage or something prior to any intention, prior to desiring or planning revenge yet nevertheless part of the arc? And what of various activities that blur the line between the inner invisible stages and the outer physical phases—especially in the theater? What of those passionate speeches, for example, especially when only the audience hears them? What is the exact status of a prayer? Further, we must be interested in the point at which a group of phases takes on significance, how a particular act or gesture becomes a meaningful part of the arc of revenge.

Since there are more things in *Hamlet* than are dreamt of in any terminology, I have taken the liberty of adding one more term to Austin's three. It is not philosophically rigorous, but I think for our purposes it provides a useful image for the way the components of an action are related. I propose to think of that arc from stage or pre-stage to stretch, from the most inward preparatory stirrings of an action to its ultimate results, as a *spectrum*, a curve broken up into many delicately shaded segments. Sometimes the segments correspond precisely to stages, phases, or stretches, sometimes not. At one end is the innermost principle of one's being, "the heart of my mystery," as Hamlet calls it, at the other end a decisive and especially significant achievement like revenge.[3]

In many revenge plays, we are likely to feel that the arc is rather simple. The obstacles to completing it lie in the physical and political circumstances of the world in which the revenger moves. The spectrum has few divisions. Deep outrage, rational planning, preliminary steps, revenge. But in *Hamlet* we are made aware of what seem to be countless dizzyingly blended bands along the spectrum. It is not only that Hamlet's own actions are labyrinthine, his motives often hard to follow. At times the relation of different portions of the spectrum seems to shift and change. Indeed the shading and discrimination of segments is so complicated that even the convenient metaphor of the spectrum becomes inadequate and we are left simply with the deeply felt sense of how difficult it is to grasp the process by which inner and outer movements coalesce into something we can give the name of action.

Let me turn to some examples. We are often reminded in *Hamlet* of a curious theatrical fact. In the theater, portentous and unintelligible gestures often seem extraordinarily interesting, because they strike us as pregnant with unarticulated meaning. The very obscurity of the outer movements directs our thoughts to the inner. The Ghost's gestures are of this kind, and Horatio, who has been among the Ghost's on-stage audience, makes explicit their suggestion of an undelivered message:

> Yet once methought
> It lifted up it head and did address
> Itself to motion like as it would speak.[4]
> (I, ii, 215-17)

There is also Ophelia's description of Hamlet's behavior at the beginning of the second act, to which she has been sole witness. Here, the meaning of the gestures she has seen—the true state of Hamlet's mind—remains cloaked in an ambiguity which centuries of critical and theatrical interpretation have done nothing to dispel:

> He took me by the wrist and held me hard;
> Then goes he to the length of all his arm,
> And with his other hand thus o'er his brow
> He falls to such perusal of my face
> As 'a would draw it. Long stayed he so.
> At last, a little shaking of mine arm,
> And thrice his head thus waving up and down,
> He raised a sigh so piteous and profound
> As it did seem to shatter all his bulk
> And end his being.
> (II, i, 87-96)

Note, too, that here Hamlet, staring perplexedly at Ophelia, seems himself concerned with the pregnant opacity of appearance.

Much later in the play, Ophelia's madness provides another reflection on the process which, in Austin's terms, may be described as the way the obscure phases of an action arouse a desire on our part to interpret the stages—the intentions and feelings—behind them:

> Her speech is nothing,
> Yet the unshapèd use of it doth move
> The hearers to collection; they yawn at it,
> And botch the words up fit to their own thoughts,
> Which, as her winks and nods and gestures yield them,
> Indeed would make one think there might be thought.
>
> (IV, v, 7-12)

And to the members of the court, Hamlet's antic disposition is another example of acts that seem obscurely to imply a movement of the spirit, which they go round about to discover. In their efforts they introduce many shifts and subtle divisions into the spectrum, including the play's many analyses—too familiar to require discussion here—of play-acting, madness, and pretense.

There are, in fact, dozens of passages in *Hamlet* which play with movement along the spectrum in a subtle and provocative fashion. Their effect of course is not to make us pause and reflect on a philosophical problem, but taken together they create an atmosphere of response, a tendency to regard action in a problematic light. One tiny example I particularly like is Hamlet's account of how he forged Claudius' commission to the King of England:

> Or I could make a prologue to my brains,
> They had begun the play. I sat me down,
> Devised a new commission, wrote it fair.
>
> (V, ii, 30-32)

In these few words, there is a nice discrimination of stages, which makes for a complex mental map, not to say a bewildering one. A *prologue* is sent to the *brain*, which then begins a *play*. Except that the brain, as Hamlet tells us, began the play before the prologue. Moreover, by calling his activity a play, Hamlet blurs the line between inner and outer, since the word suggests both the text for performance (his plan of action) and the performance itself (the steps he took). The phases Hamlet describes are sitting down, devising the commission, and writing it fair. But "devising" also blurs the line. Is "devising" a thought or a deed? Does it mean having the general idea of a new commission, imagining it in detail, or actually writing it out? It suggests a rough draft of some kind, physical or mental, in which actual phrases are in some way produced, if only by being whispered under Hamlet's breath. My point again is simply that, as so often in the play, our mind is gently urged to move back and forth on the spectrum's arc.

There are really two kinds of effect we must be aware of here. One, which I am emphasizing in this essay, is the insistence on how difficult it can be to analyze action into its components, to grasp it as a process. The other is to make us sensitive to the difficulties involved in attaching a clear interpretation to human action. Our awareness of the spectrum is related to our own efforts to interpret the action of the play, a particularly complicated one, with its indirections, windlasses, and assays of bias. We struggle to discern among the countless occurrences on stage a single informing manifestation of the spirit, that is, to make a unified action out of the activity we see. This process, of course, is paralleled by the *poiesis* described in my introduction, the leading actor's efforts to suggest a single spirit for Prince Hamlet in the face of the part's immense variety, its mercurial transitions of activity and mood. The great difficulty in playing Hamlet is to suggest an agent so constituted that all these activities may be understood as his action. The entire history of Hamlet in performance testifies that the basic problem for the actor in this role, above all others in the repertory, is to find, as Sir John Gielgud has put it, "a complete basic character in which the part may progress in a single convincing line."[5]

The effort of alignment, the struggle to uncover agency in a host of fragmentary phases and stages—bits of behavior, pieces of inner life—is echoed and given richness of implication by Shakespeare's treatment of the spectrum of action. The spectrum's presence is powerfully felt in a very important passage which I shall take as my final example, the scene in which Hamlet discovers the King at prayer. Attempting to pray, Claudius analyzes what he is doing very carefully, in terms of motivation, thought process, words, gestures, and results, and he makes us sharply aware of how many points there are on the arc, especially at what might be called the inner end of the spectrum. Inclination, will, repentance, thought, and prayer itself, are all parts of a single action whose ultimate stretch is an effective petition to God:

> Pray can I not,
> Though inclination be as sharp as will.
> My stronger guilt defeats my strong intent,
> And like a man to double business bound
> I stand in pause where I shall first begin,
> And both neglect . . . .
> What then? What rests?
> Try what repentance can. What can it not?
> Yet what can it when one cannot repent? . . .
> Bow, stubborn knees, and, heart with strings of steel,
> Be soft as sinews of the newborn babe. . . .
> My words fly up, my thoughts remain below.
> Words without thoughts never to heaven go.
> (III, iii, 38-98)

From thoughts to words to heaven, the action of prayer involves creating an arc that will connect all three. And yet the connection cannot come unless something deeper in the spirit than either inclination, will, or thought initiates the process. Without genuine contrition, none of the other stages can have effect. Claudius, of course, mistakes the mechanics of repentance, as any well-instructed Elizabethan would recognize. He fails to understand that repentance depends on the most deeply and thoroughly private of inner movements. Yet from a Christian point of view it is the most important action an individual can perform, whose ultimate stretch is salvation.

At the end of Claudius' speech, Hamlet's sudden appearance disturbs the much simpler alignment of motive and action that we as audience expect from a revenge drama. The hero suddenly has an opportunity for revenge thrust upon him at an inappropriate moment in the play's action.[6] We are panting for a satisfying resolution of the revenge situation, but not here, not like this, not from a chance encounter, not with a stab in the back, and certainly not in the middle of the play. It should also be observed that, as if to further disconcert us, Hamlet himself stops to ask whether this is the right moment to kill the King. He reflects on the kind of resolution his revenge requires, once more raising to our consciousness the spectrum of action. Where Claudius has been preoccupied with the stages of what he is doing, Hamlet is preoccupied with the stretches. Will Claudius go to heaven or hell? Does revenge mean killing the King under any circumstances? Or does it mean sending him to an appropriate end? Finally, our sense of the difficulty of interpreting action is heightened when we perceive that Hamlet, having looked at what the King is doing, has misunderstood the action he is witnessing. Claudius' soul is not safe at this moment but in the greatest danger: we know this because we have heard his monologue. The King's act has a relish of salvation in it only to a misinformed observer.

Shakespeare is developing a motif that had already intrigued him a year or two earlier in *Julius Caesar*. In both plays, the failure to understand the private springs of action corresponds to a similar failure to grasp the drift of action in the public world. And in *Julius Caesar* as in *Hamlet*, the two types of failure comment on each other. *Julius Caesar* begins with several scenes in which men confidently meddle with the tide of affairs. Marcellus and Flavius plunge into the celebrating crowd and persuade it to disperse, a maneuver they imagine will help check Caesar's power. Caesar listens to the soothsayer's warning and then decisively dismisses him. Brutus plans to murder Caesar for the good of the state. Each action rebounds on the initiator. And in similarly mistaken fashion, the characters misjudge each other's behavior and fail to understand the inner life behind it. Brutus fatally misjudges Antony, and lacks even Caesar's elementary insight into Cassius' motivation. Cassius himself misreads Brutus as surely as Hamlet misreads Claudius at prayer. After their first interview, he speaks of Brutus with a wondering disdain:

> Well, Brutus, thou art noble; yet I see
> Thy honorable mettle may be wrought
> From that it is disposed; therefore it is meet
> That noble minds keep ever with their likes;
> For who so firm that cannot be seduced?
>                                          (I, ii, 306-310)

But Brutus has not been wrought from what he is disposed to do. His psychology is not as Cassius has guessed—and though Cassius does, in fact, seduce him, to his own and Rome's great loss, it is for reasons neither of them ever understands.

For Shakespeare in these plays, the problematics of action on the stage-phase level seem linked to the great public problem of how one acts meaningfully in a world whose "events" remain "invisible." For the political man must enter into a skein of cross-purposes so complex that he can never see where his actions are carrying him, can never see that his actions will place a Fortinbras or an Octavius on the throne, an Alexander in a bunghole. That uncertainty about results is an absolute condition of the *vita activa*.[7]

Compelled, against their will, to political violence, both Brutus and Hamlet struggle to find a basis for action consonant with their sense of human value and the dignity of mind. Hamlet is of course far more aware that the nature of action is itself in question. Equally important, his play, unlike *Julius Caesar*, involves its audience in dubieties about the actions it is witnessing, elusive questions about where the play is going, where its hero is coming from.

Struggling to pray, the King has reminded us of a perspective on action very different from our own or that of the characters:

> 'Tis not so above.
> There is no shuffling; there the action lies
> In his true nature.
> (III, iii, 60-62)

In the prayer scene, we become freshly aware that, privileged as we are as theatrical spectators, we have not yet achieved such a godlike view of the action of the play. Action in its true nature is hard to grasp.

Claudius finally tries to make his knees bend in order to stimulate the thoughts necessary for a true act of repentance, a backward movement along the spectrum from external phase to inner stage that Hamlet will later recommend to the Queen:

> Assume a virtue, if you have it not . . .
> For use can almost change the stamp of nature.
> (III, iv, 161-69)

At the play's end, Hamlet at last finds a satisfying action in which there is no shuffling—though it requires shuffling off the mortal coil. He finds it in two respects. First, as part of a providential plan, it achieves a large and unambiguous moral clarity, larger and clearer than anything Hamlet has been able to accomplish through the unaided exercise of his will. Having decided to "let be," he is enabled by a series of accidents to force the King to swallow the drink the King himself has poisoned and stab him with his own envenomed sword. The guilty man dies by his own criminal instruments, in a manner that makes his guilt plain to all. Secondly, the ending is satisfying from the point of view of the audience. Our *theoria* switches gear in the last few minutes into a mode closely resembling that of a fast-paced adventure drama. The fencing scene is splendidly active, suddenly and swiftly resolving in effect.

But it's a kind of sublime trick. The heroic elation communicated by the virtuoso ending simply gives us a new peak of energy from which to contemplate the ambiguities of the action spectrum. Even while sweeping us along to a decisive climax, the last moments of the play flash before our minds several competing ways of construing the play's action. Hamlet begs Horatio to stay behind to tell his "story"—and we may well wonder what this story might be. The frequent literary retellings of it (especially those like Cavafy's that alter nothing in Hamlet's life but the interpretation of it) suggest that its events can be parsed into many actions.

Horatio's version, we know, will be that of the "sweet prince," but this may not be how the English ambassadors will see him. Fortinbras' story of Hamlet presents him as a noble soldier—or at least that is the version he chooses to make public. And of course by giving Fortinbras the last word, the play draws our attention to the most disturbing stretch of Hamlet's action, which makes his tale read rather differently—Hamlet's revenge has undone his father's greatest victory and placed the son of his chief enemy on Denmark's throne. Even this does not exhaust the play's destructive analysis of the spectrum of action. For Fortinbras' career has been marked by a very strongly delineated sequence of stage, phase, and stretch: (1) the intention to recover his father's right in Denmark; (2) a vigorously pursued military campaign; (3) installation as Denmark's king. Yet there is no way we can call this sequence an action. The play's concluding lines ring out clearly and resolvingly from the mouth of its simplest, most successful, most clear-cut "man of action"—but we know his life story to be no more than an opportunistic sliding from event to event.

## II

No speech in *Hamlet* is more difficult to act than the soliloquy which begins, "To be or not to be." And no speech allows us to see *Hamlet*'s analysis of action more vividly *as* action, carried on simultaneously by actor, character, and audience. In fact, the difficulty of the soliloquy springs not from its fame, as one might expect, but from the complex sense of action it imposes on us and the complex action it requires of the performer. It is worth looking carefully at the actor's problems here, first, because they have never to my knowledge been accurately described,[8] but more importantly because their solution does much to shape our interpretation of action in the play. I do not mean simply that the speech offers a commentary on the nature of action, but that the action of the speech itself—the *poiesis* of the actor fused with the *praxis* of the character—revises our own sense of action, our feelings about action in the play and in the world. It changes the rhythm of the actions we are witnessing and changes our relation not only to the action of *Hamlet* but to our desire, as an audience, to experience action, to interpret and draw sustenance from it.

At first glance, "To be or not to be" seems theatrically inert in a way the other soliloquies in the play are not. They, for instance, offer ample opportunity for those constant shifts of attack so typical of the role:

> Who calls me villain? Breaks my pate across?
> Plucks off my beard and blows it in my face?
> Tweaks me by the nose? Gives me the lie i' th' throat
> As deep as to the lungs? Who does me this?
> Ha, 'swounds, I should take it.
> (II, ii, 578-82)

Both the shift of attack and the acceleration are typical, and they are hard to find in the third-act soliloquy. If all acting is sustained by some flow of aggression, this soliloquy seems to lack obvious resources for unleashing and varying the aggressive current. The other soliloquies, for example, all begin with the release of emotions directed toward characters who have just left the stage, and they usually dramatize the speaker:

> Oh what a rogue and peasant slave am I!
> Is it not monstrous that this player here . . .
>
> (II, ii, 555-56)

"To be or not to be," on the other hand, begins with a dauntingly abstract and undirected phrase.

Indeed, I have never seen it done well on the stage—though I believe it can be. And the accounts of the great Hamlets of the past indicate that even the best actors have solved the problem by rather bogus efforts to convey furious cerebration—knitted brows, fixed stares, and the like—with, at least in the case of Booth, a galvanic overreaction on "perchance to dream!" Even the greatest, Garrick and Macready, seem to have pulled some damnable faces here, which suggests an attempt to jazz up a passage they perceived as static.[9]

The problems are intriguing, and, before looking at them, let me offer two guidelines and a caveat. In studying the speech it will be useful to be on the lookout for histrionic patterns that are present in the other soliloquies and elsewhere in the part. Great dramatic roles frequently repeat certain characteristic gestures of performance, figures of self-projection or self-presentation which lend themselves to the actor's effort to project his character to the audience. In the role of Hamlet, in addition to the histrionic motifs already mentioned—acceleration and shifts of attack—two stand out. One is that in the other major soliloquies there is a buried current of emotion that takes its time working to the surface, but is active beneath the surface earlier. An example is Hamlet's horrified memory of his mother's remarriage in the first soliloquy, which he fights to keep suppressed. The other feature to look for is Hamlet's habit of gathering his feelings into rapidly moving lists which carry an emotional progression:

> all trivial fond records,
> All saws of books, all forms, all pressures past.
>
> (I, v, 99-100)

Both these habits translate Hamlet's inner life into sharply profiled expressions. Their presence, to any extent, in the third-act soliloquy would be of great help to the actor.

As for the caveat, it is perhaps obvious, but I would urge that it be kept firmly in mind, since it applies to all discussions of performance in this book. There are dozens of ways to read the lines of any rich dramatic speech effectively. In what follows, I shall have to opt for particular readings, as an actor does, and ignore others perhaps equally valid. I hope my readings will be entertained at least for the sake of argument, because, in most cases, the main points I am making about them apply to the other readings as well. They illustrate the presence of larger histrionic patterns and devices which make themselves felt—and whose meanings remain substantially the same—over a very wide range of possible local readings.[10]

With that let me turn to the speech itself:

> To be, or not to be: that is the question:
> Whether 'tis nobler in the mind to suffer
> The slings and arrows of outrageous fortune,
> Or to take arms against a sea of troubles,
> And by opposing end them. To die, to sleep—
> No more—and by a sleep to say we end
> The heartache, and the thousand natural shocks
> That flesh is heir to! 'Tis a consummation
> Devoutly to be wished. To die, to sleep—
> To sleep—perchance to dream: ay, there's the rub,
> For in that sleep of death what dreams may come
> When we have shuffled off this mortal coil,
> Must give us pause. There's the respect
> That makes calamity of so long life:
> For who would bear the whips and scorns of time,
> Th'oppressor's wrong, the proud man's contumely,
> The pangs of despised love, the law's delay,
> The insolence of office, and the spurns
> That patient merit of th'unworthy takes,

When he himself might his quietus make
With a bare bodkin? Who would fardels bear,
To grunt and sweat under a weary life,
But that the dread of something after death,
The undiscovered country, from whose bourn
No traveler returns, puzzles the will,
And makes us rather bear those ills we have,
Than fly to others that we know not of?
Thus conscience does make cowards of us all,
And thus the native hue of resolution
Is sicklied o'er with the pale cast of thought,
And enterprises of great pitch and moment,
With this regard their currents turn awry,
And lose the name of action.
(III, i, 56-88)

What Shakespeare is imitating in this soliloquy is the action of the mind, but not that of the mind working toward a practical decision or judgment. It is what Aristotle would have called contemplation, a play of mind whose end is itself. It is colored by the experience and emotional history of the speaker, as we shall see, and it reflects decisions and judgments he has already made, but his aim is not to make a change in the world nor even, primarily, to express his feelings about it. It is to follow where his reflections may lead. Hamlet is not asking, should I bother to commit suicide? or what shall I do about the play tonight? or even, is it worth killing Claudius? He is doing just what his words say he is doing, speculating on the nature of human action.

Let us now consider the opening line, "To be or not to be, that is the question." Remember, we are concentrating on its histrionic articulation. Thematically, there is no problem. One could write volumes—volumes continue to be written—on the way these words resonate with the ideas and motifs of the play. But as a phrase for an actor to speak, "To be or not to be" is so abstract that it is in danger of being dramatically dead. Unless we can say where it comes from or what it is doing, how it contributes to the aggressive flow between actor and world, we cannot find its histrionic life.

Can the words "That is the question" help us? A soliloquy from *Julius Caesar* provides a clue, for in the second act Brutus uses an almost identical phrase in his reflections:

It must be by his death; and for my part,
I know no personal cause to spurn at him,
But for the general. He would be crowned.
How that might change his nature, there's the question.

(II, i, 10-13)

"There's the question" functions here to identify the preceding phrase as the intellectual nub of the issue. Brutus is saying, *there's* what the problem I've been going over boils down to. And this seems to be the function of Hamlet's "That is the question," with the crucial difference that Shakespeare brings us in in mid-process. We do not know what is being boiled down, and we can only feel the issue beginning to emerge as we move on through its further refinements.

"To be or not to be" is, then, what it boils down to when you consider whether it is nobler to suffer or act—whether to stay on the inner end of the spectrum, "in the mind," or to push on into the outside world. The opening attack for the actor turns out to be relatively simple. We come on Hamlet at the moment of resolving a reflective tangle about the nature of noble life, and this leads him to other, obscurer tangles. Summarizing, he expands on the neatly balanced "To be or not to be" in another pair of opposed statements: "to suffer/ The slings and arrows of outrageous fortune/ Or to take arms against a sea of troubles." But the balance is unstable, for the second part does not quite respond to the first. Taking arms against a sea is not quite the antithesis of suffering slings and arrows. It is true that "to take arms" carries on the image of a mind besieged and under military attack, but instead of moving out into the enemy camp, it enters the much less combatable "sea," and with a further dissolving of the clear imagery of action, it concludes in an abstraction so general as to be passive in effect: "And by opposing end them."

The imbalance does not make for neat logical opposition, but it does make for forward movement and for yet another instance of that constant shifting of ground so typical of the role and the play. The dramatic reason for the imbalance, and the thing that gives it histrionic life, is that each of the two opposed ideas reflects the presence of a different buried current of emotion.

For here also, though more subtly than in the other soliloquies, Shakespeare makes dramatic use of hidden emotion working its way to light. Instead, however, of exploding into view, as in "Heaven and earth, must I remember?" (I, ii, 142-43), these buried currents tend to remain below the surface, roiling and redirecting the flow, blocking and mingling with each other. There are at least three at work in the speech, and by following them we shall find it easier to chart the action of successful performance. This will, I hope, become clearer when the speech is discussed in detail, but I would like first to characterize in a more general way the acting process that seems to be both required and enabled by the soliloquy. A sense of overall histrionic effect will make it easier to appreciate the play of the details.

Put briefly, the key to the actor's performance in "To be or not to be . . ." is a kind of inner focus that allows all of Hamlet's recent experience to be present as an ever-varying pressure on his abstract speculation. Focus of this sort is familiar enough in modern drama (though rarely in connection with soliloquy or abstract thought), but at the time *Hamlet* was first performed, no Elizabethan play had ever demanded such an intensity of inward concentration. Marlowe and Shakespeare had rapidly expanded the possibilities for presenting inner life on stage, but they had always allowed the actor to chart his course of thought by a series of assaults—at least in imagination—upon the outside world, as in Hamlet's other soliloquies. Here, though, was a map drawn with entirely new coordinates. If Burbage did it well, the speech must have struck its first audience as an unprecedented example of man thinking.[11] For most of its length it floated free of external stimuli, and yet the very abstractness of its materials placed a special demand on concreteness in performance. It was always, as man thinking must always be, *this* man thinking.

Now, in one sense, the quality of the actor crucially required here is simply that typical of Hamlet as a whole—interpretation, the creation of Gielgud's single line. But in this instance the problem is not caused by variety of practical activity but by its absence. Without any significant objects to relate to, the actor must find and project an inner life that can make sense of—be strong and volatile and unitary enough to account for—the ways that Hamlet's speculation shifts and ranges. From the soliloquy's opening words, the actor is forced to move among colossally abstract concepts, words with no simple connection to experience and whose connection to each other often sounds balanced and clear-cut but is, in fact, asymmetrical and dizzyingly oblique. He must move decisively but without vulgar simplification (avoiding "solutions" which vitiate the complexity of the speech by slanting it toward a practical objective—Hamlet is afraid of death, Hamlet is contemplating suicide, Hamlet is reading from a book, etc.). He must move as this extraordinarily burdened mind moves in a moment when it is free of urgent stimulation from the outside, free of the need to act, free of audience, free, that is, of anything but its history and its powers.

Properly performed, the speech should give us a sense of thought as itself alive, moving within the actor's body like another character in the labyrinth of Elsinore. It is perhaps Hamlet's own awareness of this movement—hidden, darting, twisting to the side—that brings to his mind whips and rubs, the coils of snakes and currents turning awry. Our impression should be of a very concrete exploration of a very *general* subject. We feel one mind at one moment ranging rapidly, with sharp turns and checks, over an entire abstract field: the possibilities of human action.

It will be noticed that there exists a strange tension between the content of the speech and the moment-to-moment achievement of the actor in overcoming its problems. The actor imparts dramatic thrust to his apparently anti-histrionic materials by projecting the impression of a specific man thinking. By his action before us, the actor creates a coherent center of meaning—but he does so in the very act of insisting that action *cannot* unfold itself coherently, that it must dissolve into endless residues of thought which compromise it even as they try to grasp it. We shall shortly see how Shakespeare makes a powerful dramatic irony out of this paradox of unrevealing revelation.

As the speech progresses and we feel the spectrum of action dissolving in its own thrust toward definition, we are likely to feel also that what is driving the definition are Hamlet's own recent discoveries about the spectrum. For what the actor draws on to make the speech play is essentially the sum of a series of shocks that Hamlet has received about the sources, aims, and ends of human action—his own, his family's, his friends', and possibly Ophelia's. These are what switch his mind around at the soliloquy's points of imbalance, disturbing the surface order of contemplation, throwing the actor's body and voice into unstable relation with his words. With this kind of histrionic process in mind, we can return to a detailed examination of the speech, prepared to follow the buried currents which drive it.

I have said that at least three such currents may be discerned. The first of these seems to be associated with *bearing*—"bear" occurs three times in the soliloquy—and is accompanied by imagery of passive suffering: whips, scorns, slings, arrows, pangs, wrong, contumely. Revealingly enough, the whole panorama of human activity is now seen by Hamlet as the bearing of blows and insults. The second current, which first appears in the middle of the fifth line, "and by opposing end them," is associated with the peace of no sensation, with the obliteration of thought and feeling as itself a pleasurable goal—end, sleep, death, quietus.

Already with the appearance of a second current we come upon the basic pattern that should guide the actor in performance: an emotional current diverting the speculative movement, speculation picking up the emotional suggestion until it crosses another emotional track and is diverted or dissolved. At the beginning, as Hamlet moves away from the imagery of passive suffering ("slings and arrows"), his description of action ("take arms") becomes entangled in the imagery of peaceful surrender ("To die, to sleep . . ."). The actor must appear to be swung back and forth between the two currents, from peace to suffering ("and by a sleep [peace] to say we end/ The heartache, and the thousand natural shocks [suffering]/ That flesh is heir to!") until he trips another wire and a third current races through him. The new current springs from a source in Hamlet's recent experience which, perhaps above all others, the actor must keep in sharp focus in order to give us the sense of a specifically conditioned mind grappling with the problem of action. We feel it first at, "To sleep— perchance to dream: ay, there's the rub."

The imagery of a "rub" in bowling suggests a ball turning off course by encountering an obstacle, a bump, say, or a piece of straw on the smooth bowling surface. This provides a model for what happens to action in this speech and indeed in much of the play. But the twist in Hamlet's thought here, the new buried current of emotion, comes from his thinking about the strangeness of the unknown—life after death, the undiscovered country. We tend to underemphasize the fact that Hamlet is a man who has had a close encounter with an alien being. His response to the Ghost is not only to the news of Claudius' crime and the obligation to revenge—it is to the tremendous mystery he has glimpsed. With the instinct of the expert horror writer, Shakespeare makes his ghost something like what the audience might expect, but not quite, and hedges him in mystery. Hence, he fails to conform to either Protestant or Catholic specifications, and gives a vivid but eclectic and incomplete account of the quasi-purgatorial world in which he wanders. It is not perfectly clear whether he is a ghost or a good or evil angel. Shakespeare is not being heretical, but it is no heresy to suggest that we do not know everything about the world beyond our mortal scope.

Surely this is the reason why old Hamlet's ghost has for so long puzzled those specialists who have patiently gotten up the subject of Elizabethan pneumatology. Ghosts were a matter, not unlike ESP or extra-terrestrial visitors today, about which reasonable men might suspect some possible truth, though dubious as to the value of any particular sighting. Horatio, an educated man, defers judgment. When, after seeing the Ghost, Hamlet says, "There are more things in heaven and earth, Horatio,/ Than are dreamt of in your philosophy" (I, v, 166-67), this is no rebuke to the narrow tenets of a philosophical system—stoicism, say—but a general recognition of the metaphysical ignorance and mystery in which we move. From the first act on, the actor who plays Hamlet will find much in his part that reflects the shock to his imagination that his close encounter has given him. For me, one of the most wonderful lines in the play, a single lyrical phrase that Hamlet flings out in the midst of his horror and revulsion after the Ghost has left him, comes on the heels of Horatio's "Oh day and night, but this is wondrous strange!" Hamlet replies, "And therefore as a stranger give it welcome" (I, v, 164-65).

We can note one effect of this experience in Hamlet's treatment of suicide. In the first soliloquy, the reason why suicide is unthinkable is the everlasting canon. The boundaries of this and the other world are clearly marked. By "To be or not to be," the reason has changed: it is now fear of the unknown, the fear of something after death.

The three currents of emotion that I have mentioned—the suffering of injuries, the peace of no sensation, the shock of the unknown—may all be felt in the line about the sleep of death, "When we have shuffled off this mortal coil." *Coil* can mean noise and turmoil and also something that coils around one, perhaps like a skin, a meaning which *shuffled* reinforces. *Shuffled* is another of those evasive, sideward-moving action words with which the soliloquy abounds. The action suggested now seems both muffled and snakelike. With proper concentration on Hamlet's past, the actor can give it both the asperity of his distaste for life at Elsinore and his wonder at the perspectives the Ghost has opened for him (which perhaps prompts an irony at his own ignorance). And yet the phrase is a sufficiently peaceful, unresisting way of describing death. The overall effect—no matter what specific spin the actor puts on it, as long as he gives it full flavor—is to mix activity, apprehension, mystery, and passivity.[12]

Next, Hamlet turns away from the mystery to catalogue the whips and scorns of time, and for once we come upon the characteristic rushing and stopping movement of the other soliloquies. The survey of the oppressor's wrong, the proud man's contumely, etc., stops at the bare bodkin—there is a brief suggestion of peace at "quietus"—and then starts up again with a repetition of the "who would bear" formula. This sweeping forward and stopping allows us to feel the force of Hamlet's current view of human life as suffering; it takes over his thought. Nevertheless, it is a surprisingly detached view, a view of other people's lives. Hamlet, as Kittredge pointed out, is not contemplating his own suicide. The insolence of office, the law's delay, the proud man's contumely—these are not the difficulties of a prince. As I see it, Hamlet is asking, why don't ordinary men, given the native horror of their lives, kill themselves? He can imagine only one answer: fear of the unknown. The exclusions his logic makes are disturbing, but they should be seen for what they are. Hamlet is not expressing suicidal depression at this point, but a bitterly perplexed vision of human action.[13]

Hamlet goes on to link his reflections to his own situation. He does this by generalizing them to include all mankind. He moves toward statements like, "Thus conscience does make cowards of us all." But this movement toward generalization, like the movement toward action in the speech, is affected by an obscuring sideward displacement. Hamlet, for instance, describes the will not as stymied or even weakened, but as "puzzled," a word, for Elizabethans, with associations of distraction, confusion, darkness, bewilderment. Shakespeare himself uses it twice elsewhere—Cleopatra's presence in battle is said to puzzle Antony, that is to distract him, divert his attention, and in *Twelfth Night* Malvolio is described as more puzzled than the Egyptians in their darkness. The impression is not of a process coming to a halt, but rather of its being diverted into mysterious channels.

After having summed up, "*Thus* conscience does make cowards of us all," Hamlet shifts ground and applies his observation not to ordinary men but to the scene of high action. To do so, however, he does not use an image of the effects of cowardice as we normally understand them. He does not evoke the abandonment of an enterprise, a dead stop, turning tail—but again the feeling of diversion, of a flow twisting off course, the loss not of action but of action's name:

> And enterprises of great pitch and moment,
> With this regard their currents turn awry,
> And lose the name of action.

Thus, in these last words, we move backward or inward on the spectrum. An action's name—its significance or reputation or meaning—is somehow lost in the diverted flow of the action itself.

It is a wonderfully teasing conclusion to a restless, twisty speech. And I wonder if I am right to hear something of Hamlet's typical irony here, this time addressed more directly to the audience than anywhere else in the play. For in the closing lines of the soliloquy Hamlet seems to take one more step back, even as he contemplates the action about to break loose in Elsinore, the action we are contemplating, guessing about, and—as befits the audience at a tragedy—expecting to receive with utmost seriousness. Surely, I hear him saying, you are looking forward to an enterprise of high significance, of great pitch and moment. You have seen me plan it thus in the previous scene. And yet . . . what is it you expect of action? If action is as self-dissolving as Hamlet feels it to be—as he has *acted* it for us in his soliloquy—why are we so eagerly following the action of this play?

I think this is not fanciful, for it is exactly here, in the third act, that the questions of action raised by the play are most turned back on its audience. And I would like to conclude this essay by placing the soliloquy back into its dramatic context. In the third act of *Hamlet*, we feel we are being led up to the heart of the play's mystery, yet somehow we miss it. The active movement toward climax is at its most rapid, with the play within the play and Hamlet's scenes with Claudius and his mother, but at the same time we seem to slip past full resolution. An example from Kozintsev's film version of the play will make this clearer. There, Hamlet does *not* come upon the King at prayer; Kozintsev omits the entire scene. The effect is to simplify an arc of action that Shakespeare has deliberately made complex. If Hamlet is allowed no moment alone with Claudius, Polonius' death becomes the only reason why Hamlet doesn't get to complete his revenge after the Mousetrap. Thinking to kill the King, he accidentally stabs the wrong man, gets involved in a scandal, and is shipped off to England before he can accomplish his task. Bad luck. In Kozintsev's scenario, Hamlet's drive toward revenge seems simple and clear, if temporarily thwarted. Shakespeare instead forces an equivocal confrontation between Hamlet and Claudius before the opportunity for revenge is lost, leaving us with a more puzzled sense of the play's direction, and aware that, if we ever expected a clarity of development like that of Kozintsev's film, we have been seriously mistaken. We have seen some rapid and exciting phases of the action, but what is the action's name?

At the same time, by having Hamlet encounter the King, Shakespeare alters the rhythm of constantly going round about, of windlasses and assays of bias, of spiralling pursuit in the corridors of Elsinore, by making an unexpected cut, as it were, to the center of the plot. Hamlet, sword in hand, suddenly stands over his enemy. And the most disconcerting result of this procedure is that the sudden cut to the center turns out to be no more resolving than the roundabout movements.

It has often been pointed out that the "To be or not to be" soliloquy is itself a surprise for the audience, coming so soon after Hamlet has vigorously decided to catch the conscience of the King in the play within the play. Certainly the speech constitutes a striking break in the rhythm of his action. But there is really no break in Hamlet's readiness or resolve. It is Hamlet's habit, when awaiting any grand and dangerous moment which he can do nothing more to prepare, to pass the time in reflective speculation. Thus he reflects on reputation while waiting for the Ghost to appear, on providence while waiting for the fencing match to begin. But in this scene the reflections are unsettling because they make his readiness and resolve seem pointless, and leave the audience doubtful about assigning the name of action to his undertaking.

Our confidence in the name and nature of action is further undermined by the context Claudius has established for Hamlet's soliloquy before his nephew enters. He explains carefully to Gertrude:

> Her father and myself (lawful espials)
> Will so bestow ourselves that, seeing unseen,
> We may of their encounter frankly judge
> And gather by him, as he is behaved,
> If't be th'affliction of his love or no
> That thus he suffers for.
> (III, i, 32-37)

Then Hamlet comes in, and for a moment, the moment of the soliloquy, he is alone for *us* to spy on. The convention of soliloquy being that no one can hear the speaker except the lawful espials in the audience, Claudius' preparations have heightened our sense that this soliloquy will be a chance for us to "gather" Hamlet's state of mind from the way "he is behaved." Here, amid the increasing tangle of plots and doubts, is a chance for clarity, a privileged glimpse into the self at the center of the action. And, at first, Hamlet's speech seems to offer us exactly that. It is even more inward, in the sense of showing us more of the pure play of Hamlet's mind, than any we have yet seen. But what, finally, do we gather of him?

Not, as we might have expected, some resolving glimpse, some central revelation—but instead the portrait of a mind moving on the currents of an even larger mystery: being and not being, time, death, the unknown, the panorama of human injustice. While the movement of the speech and the concreteness it requires of the actor give us a sense of unprecedented closeness to the hero, the content leaves his inner life opaque. The last lines complete our disorientation. As we have already seen, Hamlet turns our expectations against us, undercutting our naive hopes for the pitch and moment of a clear-cut action. Coming where it does, then, the soliloquy is a troubling prelude to the dissonances and missed resolutions of the third act. Instead of revelation, it plunges us back into mysteries of our own.

For the large moral and metaphysical questions that Hamlet poses have been joined by his play to some of our most primitive anxieties—feelings which mark our first discoveries, in infancy and early childhood, of the gap between self and world. From our first moments in Elsinore, we enter an atmosphere which, though strange, is not entirely unfamiliar. Life in Claudius' castle (or does it belong to the Ghost?) is dominated by just those sources of fear and uncertainty which so quickly make a child feel isolated—darkness, cold, lies, secrets presumed to be nasty, inexplicable dumb shows and noise, the interruption of love, a mother's defection, a father's dread command. Interwoven with these is Hamlet's rational, superbly analytic voice, translating the primitive fears into their sophisticated philosophical counterparts, reminding us of mortality, the inadequacy of reason, the disappointments and falseness of daily life. In such an atmosphere, to be disoriented about the action, to have our appetite for action sharpened only to be turned against us, is to feel very personally threatened and deprived.

Thus, the device which concludes the soliloquy, its turning

of our expectations about action back against us, is of the essence of the play. It will be remembered that the initial action of *Hamlet* involves the asking of a question. It is a basic question, the first in the mind of any audience at any play, "Who's there?" The first thing Hamlet gives us, then, is our own thought, but echoed in a mood of surprised and fearful expectation in the cold, dark night by Bernardo, a soldier who thinks he has seen a ghost. Like most of the characters in *Hamlet*, like the members of its audience throughout most of the play, Bernardo is urgently questioning a sinisterly enigmatic world. The reply he receives sets up a strategy that the whole action of *Hamlet* perpetuates. Suddenly, it is his own identity that is under challenge. The movement of the question outward along the spectrum of action is reversed and turned back upon the questioner. "Nay, answer me," Francisco replies, "stand and unfold yourself." Ultimately, this is what the Ghost requires of Hamlet and his play of us.

Even that, however, may be to describe our engagement with *Hamlet* too comfortably, with something of the misplaced confidence of a Polonius. For unfolding the self can not only be a painful process, it is an agonizingly uncertain one. Inevitably, it questions its own validity, raising as it does the problem of action in an essential form. How can our doings be unfoldings? Hamlet begins his play by insisting that he has that within himself which cannot be unfolded in action; by the third act he is committed to action, but in the great soliloquy his analysis of the action-process is as baffled as it is fascinated. And when, at the end of the play, he ceases to worry about the invisible event and simply lets things be, they unfold so extensively that his mother dies and Fortinbras becomes King of Denmark. The wonderful vigor of the final scene vibrates in odd harmony, as we have noticed, with the questionable results of Hamlet's career and with the frustrating, circuitous, doubt-haunted passages by which we in the audience have reached the play's conclusion. Compelled to keep moving through this theatrical labyrinth, we re-explore both our childhood fears of being folded up so tightly we can never get out and our more adult despair that life will leave us like a peeled onion, all exfoliation and no center. If, in performance, *Hamlet* communicates an impression of heroism, perhaps it is the heroism required to stand at the center and unfold oneself, knowing not only that the center cannot hold but that it may not exist.

# III. Othello's Cause

## I

IN *Othello*, the course of the action seems all too plain. Instead of struggling, as in *Hamlet*, to make sense of what is going on, we feel compelled to stop it. "Don't listen to him!" we say as Iago talks to Othello, and "Don't do it!" as he prepares to strangle Desdemona. *Othello* is probably, of all tragedies, the one in which the audience comes closest to intervening in the action—at any performance you will hear people talking about this feeling during intermission, usually with surprise. Indeed, one reason *Othello* strikes us as such a clear and simple play is that our reaction makes us feel so strongly, so unmistakably, the direction the play is going.

How important is this reaction? Surely, one might say, it comes about simply because Iago is the most melodramatic of Shakespeare's villains. Perhaps he is, but consider some interesting comparisons. Even when Edmund is at his most melodramatic and Iago-like with his father and Edgar, my impression is that audience reaction is never so intensely interventionary. And among the less mature plays, Aaron the Moor is surely as melodramatic as Iago, but we don't feel that special tug—the almost unbearable need to break in. If we are to understand *Othello* properly as a work of the theatrical imagination, we must come to terms with this emphatically solicited response.

Now, of course it is true that other strong emotions are aroused by the play. Marvin Rosenberg, for example, points out that *Othello* has always been notable for its power to cause tears.[1] Still, even here the fact is that we see the tears coming a long way off and wish to stop the process that will cause them. We feel the possibility of tears rising through an action we yearn in vain to interrupt. That hopeless yearning— our sense that what Iago is doing to Othello is excruciating— is special to this tragedy. To understand it, though, and to understand why Shakespeare cultivates it so thoroughly, we must look with some care at the emotional pivot of the action, the point where we wish to intervene.

This point is communicated to us not so much as a place in the play's external sequence of events as a stage in the action of Othello's mind. For all its apparent simplicity, *Othello*, like *Hamlet*, elaborates a spectrum-like view of the process of human action and makes us sensitive to a problematic relation among different segments of the arc. It is particularly concerned with the sequence by which experience of events in the outside world gets translated into action based on that experience. A striking emblem of this concern may be found in a well-known phrase of Othello's which forces reader and actor alike to puzzle for a moment about the motive—the proceeding toward action—it describes. "It is the cause, it is the cause," says Othello as he prepares to kill Desdemona— and we are forced to search for the cause of this cause. We ask, as the actor must ask, not only what is this cause which Othello cannot name, but why he cannot name it and why he must so urgently focus on its existence and quality. "It," of course, refers to Desdemona's adultery, but in order for us to feel that the speech itself has been effectively caused— motivated—in performance, the actor must have discovered and convincingly participated in the cause of his belief that Desdemona is adulterous.

While the line itself is not difficult to understand, it never-theless points to a central acting problem in *Othello*, and it reflects a central concern with the nature of action in the play. The actor who plays Othello must find the cause of his cause. His jealousy motivates his rage, but Iago instigates the jeal-ousy. What causes Othello to receive the instigation? Criticism has tended to translate this question into moral terms, sug-gesting various flaws in Othello's character to account for his loss of faith in Desdemona, but we instinctively feel that such analysis is beside the point. That Othello might have behaved better is not interesting, any more than it is interesting that Macbeth or Lear or Hamlet might have behaved better. What is interesting about tragic heroes is that they behave the way they do. That Othello shouldn't have been jealous is scarcely the point of his play—but that we nearly cry out as we feel his jealousy being implanted is a good part of the point. We cry out as we feel the cause about to be caused.

It is in attempting to locate this cause that we feel the presence of a spectrum. The movement of Othello's mind as he becomes jealous involves him in a curious interplay between notions of judgment, feeling, and perception, between "knowledge" and "thought." Indeed the play's vocabulary suggests a particularly riddling concern with *thinking* and *knowing* as the roots of action—and this effect is most pronounced at the moment in the play when we feel the typical excruciation beginning. Notice that this occurs not when Iago announces his malign intentions, but later, when he first goes to work on Othello. The italics, of course, are mine:

IAGO. Did Michael Cassio, when you wooed my lady,
   *Know* of your love?
OTHELLO. He did, from first to last. Why dost thou ask?
IAGO. But for a satisfaction of my *thought*,
   No further harm.
OTHELLO.         Why of thy *thought*, Iago
IAGO. I did not *think* he had been acquainted with her. . . .
OTHELLO. Is he not honest?
IAGO.       Honest, my lord?
OTHELLO.          Honest? Ay, hones
IAGO. My lord, for aught I *know*.
OTHELLO. What dost thou *think*?
IAGO.      *Think*, my lord?
OTHELLO.         *Think*, my lor
   By heaven, thou echoest me,
   As if there were some monster in thy *thought* . . .
   Show me thy *thought*.

IAGO.     My lord, you *know* I love you.
OTHELLO.                                    I *think* thou dost;
          And, for I *know* thou'rt full of love and honesty . . .

                              (III, iii, 94-118)

Like Hamlet, Othello is aware that any significant gesture is
something that a man might play, but it doesn't trouble him,
because he *knows* what passes show—or thinks he knows:

IAGO.     I dare be sworn, I *think* that he is honest.
OTHELLO.  I *think* so too.
IAGO.                          Men should be what they seem;
          Or those that be not, would they might seem none!
OTHELLO.  Certain, men should be what they seem.
IAGO.     Why then, I *think* Cassio's an honest man.
OTHELLO.  Nay, yet there's more in this:
          I prithee, speak to me as to thy *thinkings*,
          As thou dost ruminate, and give thy worst of *thoughts*
          The worst of words.

                              (125-33)

What engages and appalls us here is the action of planting
suspicion in Othello's thought. Othello will soon "know" that
Cassio and Desdemona are lovers. He will know it by ocular
proof, but the knowledge and the proof will depend on the
thought Iago has planted.

This scene is, of course, a turning point in the play. But the
very sharpness of the turn raises a question which sheds light
on the way the play makes us feel about action. Actors and
readers alike have traditionally made much of the problem:
at what moment, exactly, does Othello become jealous? Readers are tempted to look for it, and actors must. Or at least
they must arbitrarily determine on such a point, in order to
map Othello's action persuasively. And readers are tempted
to look for it—irresistibly drawn in most cases—because of
the action of the play. The issue of Iago's instigation is so
compelling, the spectacle of what he does to Othello so fas-
cinating and appalling, the mystery of how jealousy gets planted
in the mind so central and disturbing, and the scene itself so

cunning and convincing, that one is drawn to pore over these passages, combing them for the very instant of malignant transfer. That there need be no single point—because minds may not behave that way—is no matter. Our belief that such a point must exist is part of our mythologizing of the process, one more reflex by which we honor the mystery of human action.

Here, then, is the spectrum the play insists on. It may be described as the arc through which Othello, as he prepares to execute Desdemona, imagines that his mind has moved. For he thinks he has arrived at his "cause" by a process of careful deliberation. The spectrum runs, let us say, from sight to thought to feeling to some decisive deed:

> I'll see before I doubt; when I doubt, prove;
> And on the proof there is no more but this:
> Away at once with love or jealousy!
> (III, iii, 190-92)

In this passage, thought waits on evidence and analysis. Othello won't think himself wronged until he knows it, and won't know it until it's proved. But, as Iago knows, everything can spring from thought, or rather from a small adjustment in Othello's thought which Iago can contrive to make:

> Dangerous conceits are in their natures poisons,
> Which at the first are scarce found to distaste,
> But with a little act upon the blood,
> Burn like the mines of sulphur.[2]
> (III, iii, 323-26)

Iago's little act upon the blood is the central action of the play, and it changes everything for Othello. Entering after this speech, he says:

>      'Tis better to be much abused
> Than but to know't a little.
> (333-34)

There is of course no way for Othello to know what he knows

*a little.* Or rather he gives himself away here by substituting *know* for *doubt* or *suspect.* To have Iago's suggestion in his thought is already to know it. The ocular proof which follows depends entirely on the existence of the planted thought, as is made clear by the scene in which Othello observes Cassio with the handkerchief. This, I think, is what attracted Shakespeare to Cinthio's use of that detail. The point of the handkerchief, for Shakespeare, is not that a man's happiness can be destroyed by a trifle, but that, to a mind properly prepared, a trifle can become a *proof.*

The excruciating excitement of the temptation scene, then, lies in the way it makes us aware of this delicate and irreversible implantation in Othello's mind. We know that if Iago can transfer his "thought" to Othello, even "a little," it will establish itself as prior to all the Moor's other thoughts and determine his knowledge. We suffer as we wait helplessly for that microscopic "act upon the blood" to be performed.

Similarly, we feel a version of this excitement when Othello questions Desdemona about the handkerchief:

DESD. I say it is not lost.
OTHELLO.                            Fetch't, let me see it!
DESD. Why, so I can sir, but I will not now.
     This is a trick to put me from my suit:
     Pray you let Cassio be received again.
OTHELLO. Fetch me the handkerchief! My mind misgives.
DESD. Come, come!
     You'll never meet a more sufficient man.
OTHELLO. The handkerchief!
DESD.                            I pray, talk me of Cassio.
OTHELLO. The handkerchief!
DESD.                            A man that all his time
     Hath founded his good fortunes on your love,
     Shared dangers with you—³
                    (III, iv, 85-94)

As we have said to Othello during the scene with Iago, "Don't listen to him, don't take it that way!" we say to Desdemona,

"Don't say that, don't put it that way." We can see how each of her speeches takes its place as evidence in Othello's mind, becomes part of his knowledge because of his thought. The intensity of the audience's response to *Othello* comes largely from the way we feel the play's action pivoting deep within the hero's mind.

## II

The language of *Othello* elaborates this conception of action at every turn. We have already seen how *thought, think*, and *know* echo through crucial passages. It is equally significant that in the first act Othello is much concerned with cues and hints, with processes and proceedings, with the way in which his actions rise properly from the appropriate sounding of a note:

> Were it my cue to fight, I should have known it
> Without a prompter.
> > (I, ii, 82-83)
> ... It was my hint to speak. Such was my process.
> > (iii, 141)
> Upon this hint I spake.
> > (165)

Our early impressions of Othello depend very much on his deliberateness of response, on the cue carefully inspected and met—usually after a noticeable pause—with a measured re-action.

Later in the play, the destruction of the normal arc which connects perception, thought, and action is brilliantly expressed in Othello's fourth act seizure. Here his mind throws up fragments of the arc—bits of evidence, processes of inquiry, storms of feeling, images of revenge. Causes and effects, cues and results, still concern him, but now, as his mind founders under an emotion whose source he cannot grasp, his vision of them is chaotic:

52

Lie with her? Lie on her?—We say lie on her when
they belie her.—Lie with her! Zounds, that's fulsome.—
Handkerchief—confessions—handkerchief!—To confess,
and be hanged for his labor—first to be hanged, and then
to confess! I tremble at it. Nature would not invest herself
in such shadowing passion without some instruction. It
is not words that shakes me thus.—Pish! Noses, ears,
and lips? Is't possible?—Confess—Handkerchief?—O
devil! (IV, i, 36-44)

The passage, though superficially incoherent, is psychologically very precise. Othello is raving, and in his agitation pieces
of the items Iago has planted in his brain whirl before him.
He is disturbed, not only by what he thinks Desdemona has
done—but at the fact that the thought is in his mind, disor-
dering his judgment. In his raving, he wrestles as much with
the dimly perceived causes of his thought as with the thought
itself.

Iago's words have filled Othello's mind with pictures of
Desdemona and Cassio naked together, which function for
him as ocular proof, and much of the speech is taken up with
bewildered and appalled reflections on the power of words.
To begin with, there is "lie," which has echoed down the
scene that has just taken place. To torment his victim, Iago
has substituted the brutally descriptive "lie on her" for the
euphemistic "lie with her," and Othello here expresses his
shock at both the physical image and the fact that the alteration of a single word has so disturbed him. But where we
might expect him to say, "We say lie with her when we mean
lie on her," his mind stumbles on another meaning of "lie,"
and he says, "We say lie on her when they belie her." "Belie"
in Shakespeare seems always to mean *tell lies about*, but it is
an ambiguous word, which also has the Elizabethan meaning
*to denounce as false, to give the lie to*. The antecedent of
"they" in "they belie her" is obscure, suggesting at once Desdemona's accusers, the "evidence" against her, or perhaps the
words of Iago's accusation, words like "lie." Othello goes on

to profess himself revolted, not by Iago's phrase, "lie on her," but by his euphemism: "Lie with her! Zounds, that's fulsome." He feels in the grip of "lying" here, in all its competing senses. In his mind the word has taken on a monstrous life he is helpless to resist.

Another word that obsesses him in this passage is *confess*. A confession is a series of words that explain evidence, that become evidence. Othello's breakdown is precipitated by an exchange in which Iago teases him with hints that Cassio has confessed to adultery with Desdemona, while Othello presses him to be more explicit:

> IAGO. What if I said I had seen him do you wrong?
> Or heard him say—as knaves be such abroad
> Who having, by their own importunate suit,
> Or voluntary dotage of some mistress,
> Convincèd or supplied them, cannot choose
> But they must blab—
> OTHELLO.                            Hath he said anything?
> IAGO. He hath, my lord; but be you well assured,
> No more than he'll unswear.
> OTHELLO.                           What hath he said?
> IAGO. Faith, that he did—I know not what he did.
> OTHELLO. What? What?
> IAGO. Lie—
> OTHELLO. With her?
> IAGO.                  With her, on her; what you will.[4]

(24-35)

Now, as he raves, Othello feels he has received the evidence of a confession, feels he wants it, does not want it. And so he isn't certain whether he has heard the confession, heard about it, or wishes to extract it. The idea of Cassio confessing stirs him to vengeance; he will hang Cassio ... no, he will hang Cassio to drag the confession from him. His emotion has reversed his logic, and it is so strong it makes him tremble. Or, rather, he trembles, and the ambiguous "it" ("I tremble at it") only suggests how far beyond his grasp the source of his trembling is. His response frightens and mystifies him, and yet even his paroxysm strikes him as proof of Desdemona's adultery. "Nature would not invest herself in such shadowing passion without some instruction." *Instruction* has a double possibility of meaning—it refers either to a truth which nature in its paroxysm echoes, or to an instigation like Iago's. Those horrible, fragmentary bodily images of lust or punishment—noses, ears, lips—must come from somewhere. It cannot be mere words that shake him thus—they must mean something, must they not? Below the level of consciousness, Othello is carrying on his last struggle with Iago. Even in the moment of breakdown, he is seeking for the cause of a cause.

To conclude this part of the argument, it will be useful to glance at an obscure scene which criticism has largely ignored. For even here, in a very odd and subordinate passage, the immense difficulty of knowing the right cue for action, of discriminating causes and effects, of moving correctly from perception to deed, is cunningly elaborated. The effect is all the more striking because it accompanies a very busy moment near the end of the play, when we are eager to rush elsewhere. Acting under Iago's instructions, Roderigo has ambushed Cassio, and the two have wounded each other. While they lie crying for help, Lodovico and Gratiano wander on the scene. These two Venetian gentlemen find the action before them hard to follow, and are uncertain how to act:

*Enter Lodovico and Gratiano*

CASSIO. What, ho? No watch? No passage? Murder! Murder!

GRATIANO. 'Tis some mischance. The voice is very direful.

CASSIO. O, help!

LODOVICO. Hark!

RODERIGO. O wretched villain!

LODOVICO. Two or three groan. 'Tis heavy night. These may be counterfeits. Let's think't unsafe To come into the cry without more help.

RODERIGO. Nobody come? Then shall I bleed to death.

LODOVICO. Hark!

*Enter Iago.*

GRATIANO. Here's one comes in his shirt, with light and weapon

IAGO. Who's there? Whose noise is this that cries on murde

LODOVICO. We do not know.

IAGO.                Do not you hear a cry?

CASSIO Here, here! For heaven's sake, help me!

IAGO.                     What's the matter?

GRATIANO. This is Othello's ancient, as I take it.

LODOVICO. The same indeed, a very valiant fellow.

IAGO. What are you here that cry so grievously?

CASSIO. Iago? O, I am spoiled, undone by villains.
Give me some help.

IAGO. O me, lieutenant! What villains have done this?

CASSIO. I think that one of them is hereabout
And cannot make away.

IAGO.                 O treacherous villains!
                   *[To Lodovico and Gratian*
What are you there? Come in, and give some help.

RODERIGO. O, help me there!

CASSIO. That's one of them.

IAGO.                O murd'rous slave! O villain!
                      *[Stabs Roderig*

RODERIGO. O damned Iago! O inhuman dog!

IAGO. Kill men i' th' dark?—Where be these bloody thieves?—
How silent is this town!—Ho! Murder! Murder!—
What may you be? Are you of good or evil?

LODOVICO. As you shall prove us, praise us. . . .

IAGO. Lend me a light. Know we this face or no?
Alas, my friend and my dear countryman
Roderigo? No.—Yes, sure.—Yes, 'tis Roderigo!

GRATIANO. What, of Venice?

IAGO. Even he, sir. Did you know him?

GRATIANO.                   Know him? Ay.

IAGO. Signior Gratiano? I cry your gentle pardon.
These bloody accidents must excuse my manners
That so neglected you.

GRATIANO.                 I am glad to see yo
                    (V, i, 37-9

The ironies here are complex. Our sympathies and judgments are given a very peculiar exercise. Lodovico and Gratiano stress the difficulty of judging their experience at a moment when we want them to rush to Cassio's aid, and in circumstances where their caution seems comically unnecessary. But in holding back from action, they exhibit a prudence we have wished for in Othello; the presence of Iago reminds us of that. Yet for all their prudence, Iago takes them in. All their concern for knowledge, proof, and thought fails to protect them, just as it has failed to protect Cassio. We are perhaps less likely to judge Othello as simple-minded when we see prudence itself led by the nose.

In any case, even in this scene the word "know" is put in a context which undermines our confidence in knowledge and severely questions the process by which we move from perception to deed. Like Othello, Lodovico and Gratiano look for some kind of proof, a secure ground for action, and believe they have been helped to it by Iago. When Lodovico says, "As you shall prove us, praise us," he means, "Judge us by our actions," but under the circumstances his bromide has a very tinny ring. In this play, where Iago's actions can appear honest and Desdemona's guilty, "proving" people (testing their virtue by their actions) turns out to be a very unreliable procedure. Lodovico's phrase thus resembles the equally conventional, "To thine own self be true" in *Hamlet,* in that it presents one of the play's most disturbing problems in the guise of a blandly confident cliché. Being true to oneself, as Hamlet discovers, is as elusive a process in his play as knowing people is in *Othello.*

The treatment of knowledge finds its final focus in Iago. Certainly by the time we reach the end of *Othello* we have been prepared to hear a very disconcerting resonance in Iago's last words:

Demand me nothing. What you know, you know.
(V, iii, 302)

This should remind us that Iago, quite as much as Othello, involves the audience in questions of how human actions are caused and causes motivated. Like Othello at the end, we wish to know why Iago acts, and like Othello we have to be content with mockery. For all the motive-hunting he inspires, for all the motives, reasons, and explanations he himself puts forward in the course of the play, Iago in the end stands tauntingly mute. What we know about him is at once absolutely clear and utterly obscure. Torments, we are promised, will ope his lips, but generations of criticism—some of it very tormented indeed—have not succeeded in exposing the cause of his cause.

## III

One very important element in the performance of Othello may be called the action of exoticism. That Othello is an exotic figure is a commonplace, but our strong impression that he is exotic deserves further analysis. Like any aspect of characterization in the theater, it is the result of action—on the part not only of Othello but of the actor who plays him. It is worth asking just what kind of *poiesis* produces our impression, and what Shakespeare has done to make this action possible. For our sense of Othello as exotic, especially in the early scenes, does much to create our attachment to him, our desire to protect him from Iago.

We can see the action of exoticism at work very clearly early in the play, in the single line Othello utters to prevent a street brawl between Brabantio's retainers and his own:

Keep up your bright swords, for the dew will rust them.

(I, ii, 58)

What does this sentence require of an actor? It must convincingly compel the attention of two opposing groups of armed men who are about to fight, and persuade them instantly to sheathe their swords. But the most interesting words in the sentence work against the natural rhythm of a convincing command. "Bright" distracts the speaker from the simple syntactical arc of "Keep up your swords," while "for the dew will rust them" is even more troublesome. As sound, it requires the dangerous consonantal cluster, "will rust them," whose articulation certainly does not reinforce the thrust of military command. As sense, it introduces the exotic, the precious, the fantastical in a place reserved for the quick persuasion of fighting men. Well performed, of course, these very details provide an unusually convincing image of such persuasion. They suggest Othello's ease in the situation, the size of his personality, the confidence, courage, and power which allow him to dance on the fine thread that separates command from provocation. Unthreatened by Brabantio's attack, Othello brings in the exotic to control the crisis.

"Dew" is a key word, too, for it is here that Othello's mind makes a leap which the actor's voice must follow. To think of the dew at this moment—and, more than that, to think of it as available to a poetic conceit which can be developed in the teeth of a street fight—requires and expresses a very distinctive kind of address. This, in turn, can be exhibited only through an articulation which allows the swiftly reached-for "dew" to function lucidly as subject for that slippery "will rust them"—slippery, that is, unless pronounced with the *netteté* of "dew" or "bright"—the phrase requires a command over fuzzy consonants as poised as is Othello's over the night.

The kind of performance required is what I call the action of exoticism. The actor must be able to reach for the exotic detail while keeping the arc of command, thus suggesting an Othello who can note the brightness of the swords, weave the observation into his speech with a kind of playfulness: "Look at your pretty swords"—and then move on to a phrase that transforms the moment into a magical suspension of urgency. Through the authority of the performer, the instant of frozen combat becomes the immensity of time necessary for dew to rust the swords—or perhaps we should say that the actor must make it possible for the aesthete's microscopic focus on a single drop of dew on a bright blade to be inserted into the action of the fight.

The moment is typical of Othello's way of using the exotic to command audiences. He is deliberately calling on the strange and fantastic to establish his control over the scene. But the actor—as distinct from Othello himself—must make a special effort here, and it is through the action of the performer that this kind of exoticism delivers to us an important strand of the Othello-experience. The exotic detail operates as a sign of strength because it is *reached* for—successfully. The actor demonstrates the authority of his utterance by easily incorporating elements which threaten it.

There are of course many individual readings by means of which an actor can "solve" this line. Perhaps Othello stops all motion around him by a scintilla of playful mockery in "bright," and then, with a tale-spinner's "for the bright dew will rust them," comments on the crowd of grown men he sees arrested like children in an unnecessary display of belligerence. Or perhaps he has simply, in the midst of quelling this minor disturbance, struck on a pleasingly ornamental conceit which he shares even as he goes about the easy business of command. In any case, what is both necessary and emphasized in the process is a power to relate divergent expressive elements—a structure of expression secure enough, controlled and spacious enough, to wear the exotic as a badge of security. And the actor reveals the structure by reaching out and pinning on the badge.

We see the same kind of effect displayed at length in Othello's address to the Senate. An extended analysis of this passage might note its varying degrees of exoticism. There are certainly at least three levels of exotic reference. First, phrases where the inflection departs almost imperceptibly from what we have become accustomed to think of as ordinary Venetian speech:

> Most potent, grave, and reverend signiors . . .
> 
> (I, iii, 76)

This may be Othello's dialect, his occasional slight involuntary departure from the norms he has learned. Next, there are passing elaborations of the ordinary, a word or two making strange the familiar context, like *bright* in *bright swords*:

> For since these arms of mine had seven years' pith
> Till now some nine moons wasted . . .
>
> (83-84)

Finally, there are extended sequences brought in for their exotic impact:

> The Cannibals that each other eat,
> The Anthropophagi, and men whose heads
> Do grow beneath their shoulders.
>
> (142-44)

Of course, these planes admit of many gradations, including subdued parody, in which the exotic is exquisitely mocked and yet lingered over in a fashion that is in itself another version of exoticism[5]:

> . . . What drugs, what charms,
> What conjuration, and what mighty magic,
> For such proceeding I am charged withal . . .
>
> (91-93)

As the play progresses, Othello begins to find it difficult to control these verbal gestures. The action of exoticism becomes forced, a little too willful and insistent, in the Egyptian charmer speech, and breaks down completely in Othello's fourth act fit. It is perversely and uncomfortably at play in "It is the cause . . ."; there, Othello reaches for lyric and mythological expression to try to shape and steady his emotions, but the gesture is uncertain, self-perplexed, governed by his inability or refusal, for once, to reach for a word, to name his cause.[6] Finally, when Othello recovers clarity of perception and self-command, the action of exoticism reasserts itself in the Arabian tree and medicinable gum of the suicide aria.

## IV

I have used the word "structure" to describe the kind of expression the actor who plays Othello must achieve in these passages, because I think that the action of the performer in the moments of successful exoticism allows us to experience Othello's personality as something palpably constructed, composed of elements foreign to each other, bound together by skill and power. And it is this sense of Othello which we get so strongly in the early acts—of a great self-constructor, who responds to threats by exhibiting the way he has put himself together, controlling the stage by coordinating separate and diverse components.

The operation of the performer's technique here and the operation of personality it suggests are at one with the union of domestic focus and cosmological spaciousness characteristic of the play. Like the play's verbal imagery, the impression we receive of Othello's personality suggests a combination of control and expansiveness. The unhoused free energies of the wide world with its great spaces, strange corners, and exotic violence—antres, deserts, cannibals, heavens, magic, the sea— seem placed into circumscription and confine by an action of elegant mastery. It is of course echoed in—finds its perfection in—the marriage of Othello and Desdemona.

This notion of construction and control is clearly a feature of Othello's sense of self. I think it helps explain the curious emphasis of his farewell to war:

> O, farewell!
> Farewell the neighing steed and the shrill trump,
> The spirit-stirring drum, th' ear-piercing fife,
> The royal banner; and all quality,
> Pride, pomp, and circumstance of glorious war!
> And O you mortal engines whose rude throats
> Th' immortal Jove's dread clamors counterfeit,
> Farewell . . .
>
> (III, iii, 347-54)

Why should Othello single out the "mortal engines" of war for his climax, and, more importantly, why does he describe them in such terms? Evidently, he identifies intensely with these human constructions, splendid in war, whose power (expressed as a kind of overwhelming speech—clamor from a throat) approaches the divine. And when, shortly afterward, we see Othello at his worst, we are aware of a great, deliberately constructed personality blown up by its own force.

Our sense of Othello as constructed and of the poignant vulnerability of that structure to Iago's little act upon the blood reflects an important development in Shakespearean tragedy. This is the new emphasis on the intimate connection between action and what is perhaps best called imagination, though no single term is entirely adequate. I shall use "imagination" here to denote the full range of mental activity, from rational analysis to free association, but considered in all its possible richness of invention, combination, emotional play, and intense registration of experience. The relation to action to which I refer is not readily caught in a single phrase, but it might provisionally be summed up as an impression, conveyed by all Shakespeare's great tragedies, that the field of action in tragedy and even the means of action are ultimately to be located in the imaginative life of the protagonist. The process involved must be carefully distinguished from imaginative support of action—that is, from the simpler process by which mental and emotional life either initiate action or respond to it. That Titus cries out with pain and rage at what he has been made to suffer, that, as a result, he plots revenge— these are examples of imaginative support, and they are already dramatically commonplace by 1590. What I am describing is a *fusion* of imagination and action. That Othello's world shifts violently with Iago's little alteration of his thought— and that the shift of that world is the key step in the action of the play—that is a very different and dramatically innovative relation between action and mental activity. The important issue is not to what extent actions in a play may be linked to the ideas of the protagonists instead of seeming the result of external accidents, but rather the extent to which the great events we watch are in their essentials inseparable from the shifts and struggles taking place within the imaginations of the characters who make them.

The development means everything to *Hamlet*, but in one important respect it only becomes clear in *Othello*. Hamlet is, after all, a sensitive intellectual who even has a dabbling interest in the arts. He is someone we normally think of as "imaginative." So the relation between imagination and action in his play may be a special case. But in the tragedies which follow *Hamlet*, Shakespeare chooses heroes who are, by any conventional standard, unimaginative and unreflective, men not at home in the study, who never appear with a book, who never think of themselves or appear to others as having unusually active or refined mental lives—and he boldly focuses his tragic analysis on their imaginations. By *Othello* at the latest, then, he has arrived at a new understanding of the role of imagination in tragic action: that human action flows from imagination, that our lives are essentially shaped by our imaginative constructions—that, as Stevens would say, we are conceived in our conceits.

A comparison with *Richard II* may make the point clearer. Richard is certainly imaginative; he presents himself as someone who enjoys following the flight of thought. Yet in this early exercise in tragedy, the connection between imagination and action I have been describing is never made. Richard's imagination is seen instead as an escape from the world, an excuse for inaction, as in "For God's sake, let us sit upon the ground. . . ." It is true that, as the play progresses, his power to impose his imagination, to turn it into action, seems to increase—but this is merely symbolic action, such as he achieves in the deposition scene. There he manages to embarrass Bolingbroke, but in no way diverts him from his advance to power. In prison, Richard engages reality more fully than early in the play, but now his activity is contemplative; he is again constructing a symbolic world:

I have been studying how I may compare
This prison where I live unto the world.

(V, v, 1-2)

He dies of course in an outburst of vigorous and heroic action, a release like that at the end of *Hamlet*. This final scuffle, however, is scarcely a product of his contemplation; rather, it is an escape from it.

By contrast, Hamlet, Othello, Lear, Macbeth, Antony, and Coriolanus move through their plays governed and burdened by a seething mental weight of images, conceptions, and interpretations of the world and their place in it. And out of their struggle with this burden, they act and shape their worlds. There are anticipations of this process in *Romeo and Juliet* and *Julius Caesar*, most notably in the former, where the fate of the lovers seems to flow from the imagery of their passion. But the process grows immensely in complexity and centrality from *Hamlet* on—and, in making their heroes unintellectual, the tragedies after *Hamlet* underscore the change.

We can describe this aspect of Shakespearean tragedy in another way, by considering its relation to a familiar Elizabethan habit of thought. One great source of imagery for Shakespeare and his contemporaries was the correspondence of inner and outer worlds. Emotional changes could be orchestrated by reference to changes in the world of external nature, and vice versa, while political changes could be related to both. Thus, for example, the storms and portents in *Julius Caesar* echo the turmoil in the Roman state and in Brutus' mind. But by the time of the great tragedies Shakespeare has learned to go well beyond this trope. He has transformed the correspondence of inner and outer worlds into a delicately observed process by which the mind's control over the imagery of the external world is related to its command of its inner imagery. The storm in *Lear* is not an emblem of Lear's madness. In a very precise sense, it *is* his madness. Our experience of the storm is a visit to Lear's mind, and his mind, during the scenes on the heath, is convulsed by a desperate effort to maintain that the storm's power is his own and that he in turn has power over the storm that is taking place inside him. Neither the mental nor the physical event is subordinate—the boundaries between inner and outer drama are dissolved. Lear's division of the kingdom, the contest he stages, his raging on the heath, his struggles with Regan and Goneril, his forgiveness of Cordelia, his killing of the murderer, his final words— are all equally expressions of a mental action: Lear's play-long effort to imagine himself successfully into the pain of reality.

The sense of richness of characterization we feel in the great tragedies derives largely from the manifold activity of their heroes' imaginations. We feel, as with Othello, that they negotiate between their self-conceptions and their conceptions of the world, altering both as they respond to new experiences of world and self, and also in response to other imaginations. Shakespearean tragedy lets us feel how the world is brought into being by the actions of individual imagination that sweep over it. An event takes place in Othello's mind, a rearrangement of the components by which information is construed and action constituted. This event not only propels him into action but recreates the outside world for him, alters the imagery of its encounters, changes its relation to cosmology and geography. This is not the same thing as saying Othello uses cosmological and geographical imagery to express his emotions, as Senecan heroes or Hieronymo or Titus do. Othello may seem to echo their rhetoric when he talks of the Pontic sea, but his blood is racing with a fury which springs from the releasing of an inner dam, part of the self-construction we have felt in the poise, the confident awareness of cues and hints in the first act. And later, when he says, "Goats and monkeys!" we hear not a curse, but the new inner jungle rushing out into the public world. Shakespeare has found a way to render the fact that the world of human action, the "real" world, is a mental world, a battlefield of struggling imaginations.[7]

I have said little so far about the love of Othello and Desdemona, in part because others have treated it so admirably, but primarily because I think it may be useful to see it for once in strict relation to the play's focus on Othello's mental life. For Othello's mind—in that expanded sense of his full imaginative activity—is at the center of the play. We want to interrupt the action of *Othello* because we feel his mind is being tampered with and we find the prospect unbearable. Othello's mind is a construction; Shakespeare has made it possible for us to feel the action involved in making and sustaining that construction, and we feel it all the more intensely because Othello's mind is situated at the center of a series of constructions which surround it like Chinese boxes: his public personality, his marriage to Desdemona, the Venetian world order, the cosmos. We feel the constructedness of each in the sense that we are made aware of each as holding great opposing forces in balance—black and white, sun and moon, sea and sky, Venice and Cyprus. The play makes us feel that when Iago tampers with Othello's mind he unhinges all these constructions.

The imaginative world of the play is thus designed to heighten our involvement with Othello's imagination. The sense of spaciousness and clear distinction of parts with which its cosmology and geography are endowed,[8] the fusion of "magic" and rationality,[9] of sensuality and modesty in Othello's marriage, engage us at the play's start in a grandly commanding world conception which echoes the authority of the Moor as general. These impressions convey a sense of action—of human value being established by the graceful spanning of great opposites, of a spirit that holds together in touching and majestic harmony energies that everywhere threaten chaos. Our desire to intervene in the play underlines our awareness of the fragility and value of this achievement. Our sense of Othello as a magnificent piece of self-construction both draws us to him and makes us aware of his vulnerability. And of course our protectiveness toward Othello is immensely heightened by his relation with Desdemona.

Desdemona is a remarkably realized character, but the play

sees to it that she serves above all to enlarge our awareness of Othello. The delicacy and strength of their union—their constancy and proud openness amid the compromised, clashing forces of night-time Venice—extend our impression of superb self-construction, of something deliberately put together, finely and perilously maintained. If we think of her simply in terms of our emotions as we watch the play, Desdemona is practically an image of all that is most lovely and vulnerable about her husband. Part of our desire to intervene involves a desire to protect Desdemona, but I submit that in the moment of wishing to stop Iago's instigations, we make no distinction between Desdemona and Othello. We see his reach toward exoticism in the light of his bond of faith with his wife, and see in her an instance of the perfect soul that would manifest him rightly. Both the action of exoticism, then, and Othello's union with Desdemona serve to make us feel that Iago is attacking the center of a delicate imaginative organism which encompasses Othello's mind, his career, his marriage, and his hope for grace—a seamless unity of the spheres of thought and action. We feel that in the person of Othello an entire universe of value is being threatened.[10]

When the inner construction is shattered, the outer construction falls:

My wife! My wife! What wife? I have no wife.
O, insupportable! O heavy hour!
Methinks it should be now a huge eclipse
Of sun and moon, and that th'affrighted globe
Should yawn at alteration.
(V, ii, 97-101)

In his agony, Othello discovers that he has lost a way to hold the universe together inside his head. For a moment, he thinks in terms of the conventional correspondences, and naively expects nature to parallel the disorder in his mind. But what makes the moment powerful is that we can feel the universe of the play come crashing down because Othello can no longer say, "My wife." The word "wife" is a keystone for him, something that holds his inner and his public life together, and without it, the arch falls. The action of exoticism fails. Othello reaches for divergent elements—the domestic (wife), the cosmic (sun and moon)—but he cannot gracefully join them. His hysteria, his sense that both nature and his language are failing him, contrast harshly with his earlier rhetorical ease. No longer able to wield such far-flung elements or to avoid their inner collapse, he finds the moment literally "insupportable."

At the end of *Othello*, the waters close over the hero's head as in no other Shakespearean tragedy. *Julius Caesar* and *Hamlet* were particularly concerned with the relation of their heroes to the distant and public stretches of their action. Brutus and Hamlet share a mistaken belief that they can narrowly control the results of their interventions; they think too precisely on the event. Nevertheless, one measure of both Brutus' and Hamlet's importance is the lasting effect their actions have on their nations' histories. And all the tragedies after *Othello* end with some evocation of the impact of their heroes' careers on the worlds they leave behind. Othello is granted no such echo. Compare even the civic resonance which accompanies the mourning for Romeo and Juliet. After death, their love stretches on to reform Veronese society; a golden monument will be erected in their honor. Shakespeare assures even his adolescent lovers, who care for nothing in the world beyond each other, a claim on memory he carefully denies to his great general.

At the play's end, nothing has changed in the world except that some things of value have been destroyed—a marriage, Desdemona's life, perhaps Othello's immortal soul. The lack of a public resonance only emphasizes how internal, how lonely, the disaster has been. The effect is thoroughly in keeping with the special pathos of our urge to intervene. For it is not just Othello's life or his happiness which Iago threatens but his entire being, that splendid self-definition by which he makes himself available to Venice and to us. Othello untuned is Othello no more. His occupation is gone, and the man who dies in the last act is merely he that was Othello. Before the play begins, Desdemona has seen Othello's visage in his mind, that mind whose poise and structure have enabled Othello to act and construe action, to make a space for himself in an alien world. Now, his mind having collapsed, no trace of him remains.

> The object poisons sight;
> Let it be hid.
>
> (V, ii, 363-64)

His body is not borne off, but abruptly hidden from us.

# IV. Acting and Feeling:
## Histrionic Imagery in *King Lear*

### I

SO FAR in this book, when discussing how Shakespeare writes for actors, I have tended to concentrate on the acting difficulties presented by the text, and moved directly from them to the dramatic effects which occur when they are successfully mastered. I have said little about the intervening process, by which the actor overcomes the difficulties. One might think of this as irrelevant to the playwright's art, as having simply to do with the performer's technique and talent. But the art of the playwright consists in making the exercise of that technique and talent possible—and valuable. Confronted with acting problems in a text, we are entitled to ask (1) what specific means does the text provide to enable the actor to solve its problems, and (2) how do these means contribute to the action and meaning of the play?

In this essay, I want to approach *King Lear* by focussing on the tools Shakespeare gives his leading player for solving some especially daunting problems in the title role. To do this, I shall look extensively at the role in terms of what might be called its histrionic imagery. What I have in mind when I use this phrase are various motifs of enactment Shakespeare has built into the part: mental, physical, and emotional movements the actor is called upon to make that are particularly related to his basic work of sustaining the part in performance.

Let me give an example of what I mean. The first problem that confronts an actor who wants to play Lear is gross and obvious. The part makes staggering emotional demands on the performer. The actor is required to portray a quick-tempered, eighty-year-old, absolute tyrant, who five minutes into his first scene bursts into the greatest rage of his life at Cordelia. Two brief scenes later he bursts into a greater rage at Goneril and carries on with increasing intensity for nearly a hundred lines. Next he gets *really* angry at Regan; while he is raging at her, Goneril appears and he gets angrier. His fury and outrage mount wildly until the end of the scene, at which point he goes mad. This of course is only the beginning. Three long scenes of madness still lie ahead during which, among other things, the actor has to outshout a storm. After these scenes on the heath come alternations of hallucination and murderous rage in the scene with Gloucester, the ecstatic joy of reunion with Cordelia, yet another reversal of fortune when the old king and his daughter are captured by their enemies, and finally the anguish of Cordelia's death, a scene in which the actor is required to enter literally howling and to go on from there. "The wonder is," as Kent says, "he hath endured so long," and most actors don't.

The actor who plays Lear must appear to reach an emotional extreme at the start, and then go on to greater and greater extremes. The danger is that he will soon have nothing left—not so much that he will run out of voice or physical energy, but that he will lose the capacity for discriminating his emotional response, that he will be unable to render the emotions truthfully, with freshness and particularity, and will fall into shouting or scenery chewing or playing what actors call generalized emotion, that is, some sort of all-purpose posturing. If this happens, the actor will not only be doing a great injustice to the text, he will also in a matter of moments bore his audience irremediably. Does Shakespeare do anything to help the actor with this problem?

Trained actors usually learn a variety of techniques for sustaining exact and vivid emotion in scenes of demanding intensity. One technique is to focus on a particular object. If the actor feels in danger of losing an emotion or falsifying it, he may single out a button, say, or a chair, or an eyebrow and make it the recipient or evoker of his feeling. He may direct his emotion toward the object, or find his emotion by reacting to it. In *King Lear* Shakespeare has written this technique into the title role. Repeatedly, at moments of emotional intensity, Lear will focus closely on a specific point—on an area of the body and its sensation or on a small object that produces a bodily sensation. He takes a pin and pricks himself with it; he feels the pressure of a button at his throat; he pinches himself; he holds a feather to Cordelia's mouth; he peers at Gloucester's blinded eyes; he touches Cordelia's cheek to feel the wetness of her tears; he glares at Regan's and Goneril's clasped hands; he smells and wipes his own hand; he imagines two little flies copulating; he stares at Cordelia's lips. These are all highly specific points of focus, and by playing to them and *off* them the actor is able to keep his feeling fresh. They help him to keep the performance alive, to keep the pain Lear feels coming and growing, and to keep the audience's perception of that pain vivid and exact.

These recurring gestures or movements of focus are an example of what I call histrionic images. If we were simply to consider the objects Lear focuses on by themselves, we might treat them as what are usually called poetic or dramatic images. But I am concerned with a unit of *enactment*, something Shakespeare has prescribed for the character to do, by means of which the actor projects the part. Hence, it is this repeated focussing on an area of bodily sensation that constitutes one pattern of histrionic imagery in *Lear*.

How do these images contribute to our larger experience of the play? Clearly, one of the issues *King Lear* raises is the problem of human suffering. Why do we suffer? Is there anything to be gained from it? What values can be conserved in the face of monstrous pain? These are questions the characters keep posing or addressing. And the action is designed so that we frequently find ourselves, like Edgar, believing that things cannot get any worse, only to have something happen that is more awful than anything else that has happened so far. The play's interest in suffering and endurance is plainly echoed in the problem of playing Lear and in our reaction to the performance of the role. How much more can the actor take? we ask—and the question implies, how much more can we take? A good production of *Lear* is not easy on its audience.

Now, the sequence of repeated focussings I have just described may be seen as part of the play's subtle and growing insistence on *feeling* as a source of enduring value in the chaos of cruelty and pain that threatens to overwhelm the characters, the actors, and the audience. The function of these histrionic images is, not to insist on a theme, but to engage the audience in an experience. That is, through the action of the principal actor we share the experience of discovering new precisions of feeling—moments of sympathy, tenderness, insight, or horror, for example—in spite of and indeed because of being forced to undergo scenes that strike us as unendurable and that threaten to wipe us out. They give us the sensation of advancing deeper into pain than we thought we could take, and of advancing, not into generalized empty agitation or monotony, but into profounder awareness, finer sensitivity, which could only be achieved by going this far, by having these many stages of exact response to increasing pain. And this I think is a not insignificant part of the art and vision of *King Lear*.

## II

I would like now to look at some other patterns of histrionic imagery, in which the actor is called upon to address himself to other characters, to the words he speaks, and above all to his own emotions.[1] I want especially to draw attention to the emotional and intellectual activity that all these motifs require of the actor and communicate to the audience. For, by means of these devices, Shakespeare provides the gifted actor with a set of habits and methods that allow him to relate to his own emotions, to build them, vary them, wield them, and, as we have seen, to keep them from turning imprecise or numb. This

is particularly important in *Lear* because Lear's own relation
to his emotional life is one of the great issues of the play.

We tend to think of *Lear* as a play about human suffering,
and no doubt we are right to do so. The play deliberately
overwhelms us with examples of suffering that arouse our
own most vivid fears of vulnerability to pain. How easy it is
for our eyes to be put out, how easy it would be for the ones
we trust most to betray us, how easily nature or the appetites
of others can destroy us, how true it is that things can always
get worse. But in spite of all the malice and cruelty directed
at Lear, his greatest source of suffering remains internal. The
play is less concerned with the assault upon the King from
outside than with his vulnerability to the play of his own
emotions.

Indeed, it is through Lear's early emotional outbursts that
the play first involves us in the kind of analytic awareness of
action we have noticed—with different emphasis—in *Hamlet*
and *Othello*, that is, with a problematic sense of the way inner
and outer events may be related. In the play's early scenes,
Lear seems peculiarly agitated by the connections between the
self and its acts. Like most of Shakespeare's tragic heroes, he
is inclined to work out a personal, abnormal variation on the
process that links thinking and feeling with saying and doing.
For Hamlet and Brutus, this variation takes the form of a
desire to separate the two components, to divide one's inner
life from its external manifestations—to insist with Brutus on
separating what he calls the "genius" from the "mortal instruments" (II, i, 66), or with Hamlet that whatever one's acts
may be, one has something within which passeth show. Lear
on the other hand insists on intention and action as mono-
lithically connected and on defining his own nature as powerfully and dangerously joining the two. He denounces Kent
for attempting to break the connection when Kent tries to
persuade him to revoke his decision to disinherit Cordelia,
and he uses language that insists on the leap from self to action
as something violent, powerful, instantaneous, and irresistible:

Come not between the dragon and his wrath.
(I, i, 122)

The bow is bent and drawn; make from the shaft.
(143)

Lear seems unwilling or afraid to slow down the rhythm by which he moves from intention to act. In this he resembles Macbeth, who frequently wishes to act quickly in order to escape from the pressure of his imagination. Macbeth would like to act the things in his head before he can scan them; he wants the firstlings of his heart to be the firstlings of his hand. Action for him is a way to blot out reflection and feeling. And the question of feeling, in particular, is important for both *Macbeth* and *King Lear*. In both plays, a false notion of manhood seems to struggle with the claims of feeling. The point is more easily seen in *Macbeth*. There the hero's desire to leap forward unreflectingly into action is highlighted by contrast with Macduff. After Macduff has heard that his wife and children have been murdered, he pauses before calling for revenge. He does so because, as he explains, in order to dispute it like a man, he first must feel it as a man. Macduff insists on the importance of feeling in a man's life, while Macbeth, concerned with doing all that may become a man, acts to keep from feeling. Similarly Lear, up to the storm scene, clings like Macbeth to an idea of a manly way of acting that seals one off from feeling. Confronting Regan and Goneril before Gloucester's palace, Lear, fighting against tears, calls on the gods to visit him instead with what he calls noble anger, a feeling he thinks of as more masculine:

> Touch me with noble anger,
> And let not women's weapons, water drops,
> Stain my man's cheeks.
> (II, iv, 273-75)

I imagine that the kind of anger he wants here is the type he displayed in the first scene. He is struggling to summon once more his old power to discharge violent emotional energy without suffering the full range of feeling from which his emotion springs.

Indeed, almost from the beginning of the play, Lear is fighting his feelings. Shakespeare's method of allowing the actor to play against his feelings, by repeatedly insisting, for example, that he will not weep, allows us to experience the movement of feeling toward expression as a terrifying, destructive surge. We feel it as Lear's speeches swiftly shift focus in his fight against rising sorrow:

> O, how this mother swells up toward my heart!
> Hysterica passio, down, thou climbing sorrow,
> Thy element's below. Where is this daughter?
> (II, iv, 55-57)

With this last line, he switches attention to Regan, trying to direct action and anger outward, as he has done in the first scene.

Significantly, Lear is aware in this struggle of something unnatural, but he projects it onto his daughters as he flounders in a feeling so violent and unregulated that he cannot think clearly enough even to curse or invent a revenge:

> No, you unnatural hags!
> I will have such revenges on you both
> That all the world shall—I will do such things—
> What they are, yet I know not; but they shall be
> The terrors of the earth.
> (275-79)

The power of this speech goes quite beyond its pathos, its picture of a poor old man dissolving in misery yet, like a small boy, refusing to show tears. For, in a kind of prelude to the battle with the storm that comes in the next act, Lear in battling against the mounting tears reaches into himself for a terrifying violence with which to combat them. The long-delayed onslaught of tears, the surrender to his feelings, comes on with the first noise of the storm, and it is so strong that it feels as if he were breaking into a hundred thousand pieces:

> You think I'll weep.
> No, I'll not weep.
> *Storm and Tempest.*
> I have full cause of weeping, but this heart
> Shall break into a hundred thousand flaws
> Or ere I'll weep.
> (279-83)

The actor's emotional springboard for this outburst must be found in his fight against tears, while the image of the heart breaking into a hundred thousand flaws gives him his cue for how immense the pressure of the choked-back tears must be. And now comes a dramatic stroke, very helpful to the actor, that is also an important development in the part. Unable to beat back the surge of his emotions, Lear suddenly turns his attention outside again, not to curse and rage, but to confess: "O Fool, I shall go mad!" (283). At the moment of his strongest feeling and his deepest fear, he addresses the Fool. The Fool has already become associated with the kind of feeling Lear has been resisting, that is, with acknowledged suffering. His main role has been to urge the shaming truth that Lear has made a terrible mistake about his daughters. And to Lear, someone who weeps is a fool: "Fool me not so much," he has said in this scene, "to bear it tamely" (272-73), that is, to weep. At this moment, the sudden focus on the Fool allows the actor to let Lear's suppressed feelings flash out for an instant, and the pattern of emotional release through a sudden external focus of attention will grow in importance as the play goes on. A few minutes later, out in the storm, it will be to the Fool that Lear will turn when, for the first time in the play, he acknowledges that someone else can suffer. It is thus through Lear's relation to the Fool that we first begin to feel how the experience of his own pain is being converted into keener awareness of the life around him.

### III

For the actor who plays Lear, the problem of handling Lear's emotions is inseparable from the problem of speaking the play's verse. A great deal of study has been devoted to the verse of Shakespeare's plays, but very little to verse movement and texture as part of the performance design.[2] I mean that any striking instance of technical virtuosity in a play's verse will, if the actor can master it, inevitably present itself as technical virtuosity in performance. We have already seen this with the action of exoticism in *Othello*. At this point I want to call attention to some features of the verse that Lear must speak in order to examine what actions they require of the actor. Since they are actions of speech, they will of course involve not simply vocal but also mental and emotional movement.

Lear himself has many styles of speech, many voices, more than I can investigate here. There is, for example, the riddling, shadowy voice we hear very briefly at the beginning of the play:

> Meantime we shall express our darker purpose.
> (I, i, 36)

>                                              . . . while we
> Unburthened crawl toward death.
> (40-41)

or the torrent of monosyllables in

> I will have such revenges on you both
> That all the world shall—I will do such things—
> What they are, yet I know not; but they shall be
> The terrors of the earth.
> (II, iv, 276-79)

or the eerie flickering lightness of the aria that begins "We two alone will sing like birds i' th' cage" (V, iii, 9), not to mention the various voices that mingle in the prose of his madness.

Still, all these voices have one element in common: their suggestion of the operation of some dangerously unregulable power, something not quite contained by the procedures that seek to organize it. And this is equally true of a far more prominent stylistic effect that I wish to look at in some detail. This is the presence, both in Lear's part and in others, of words and phrases that appear to be massively resistant to verse articulation, words like "tender-hefted" or "sea-monster" or "sulph'rous," which seem hard to move around in musical lines or paragraphs. What we appreciate in the music of the lines in which they appear is that the lines somehow find an energy capable of floating or swinging these densely recalcitrant chunks of meaning and sound. Of course it is really the relation of such words to the words around them that creates the impression of difficulty, just as it creates the impression of difficulty overcome. Thus, when we hear:

> Thou art a boil,
> A plague-sore, or embossèd carbuncle
> In my corrupted blood.
> (II, iv, 220-22)

or "Strike flat the thick rotundity o' th' world" (III, ii, 7), we feel that somehow words hard to move are being moved.

These words often carry a suggestion of—let me call it—monstrosity; that is, they contribute, through sound and sense, to an impression of sizable, distorted, appetitive, struggling bodies, they burgeon against the forward career of the line:

> If thou shouldst not be glad,
> I would divorce me from thy mother's tomb,
> Sepulchring an adultress.
> (II, iv, 127-29)

They seem to overflow, like an unexpected wet animal coming out of a river to snap or lap or slaver at you, or to block your path as the line goes by. Sometimes this impression is specifically carried by the sense of the word itself, sometimes by the context, frequently by the gnarled play of consonants:

> The barbarous Scythian,
> Or he that makes his generation messes
> To gorge his appetite, shall to my bosom
> Be as well neighbored, pitied, and relieved,
> As thou my sometime daughter.[3]
> (I, i, 116-20)

The movement of this passage is relatively easy, but, even so, the texture is quite unlike, say, that of Othello's equally savage but fast-moving curses or denunciations:

> Blow me about in winds! roast me in sulfur!
> Wash me in steep-down gulfs of liquid fire!
> (V, ii, 279-80)

In *Lear*, this characteristic texture is frequently achieved by using series of words linked by clashing consonants:

> If she must teem,
> Create her child of spleen, that it may live
> And be a thwart disnatured torment to her.
> Let it stamp wrinkles in her brow of youth,
> With cadent tears fret channels in her cheeks.
> (I, iv, 283-87)

Lear usually sounds remarkably different from other Shakespearean tragic heroes, even in such a simple matter as a brief explosion of rage. Take a line like "Vengeance, Plague, Death, Confusion!" (II, iv, 92.) Othello typically bursts out on a single note of fury or revulsion: "Goats and monkeys!" or "O Devil, devil!" or "Damn her, lewd minx, damn her!" Hamlet, even in his rage, uses language that multiplies distinctions in series of swiftly linked analytical variations:

> Bloody, bawdy villain!
> Remorseless, treacherous, lecherous, kindless villain!
> (II, ii, 586-87)

Lear instead breaks out in four successive, sharply separated calls for sweeping violence. Each is different, each involves, as it were, a going back to the beginning and imagining a new, more violent outbreak of destruction: "Vengeance! Plague! Death! Confusion!"

We can now see some of the characteristic action of performance that this verse texture requires of the actor. Put simply, the testing necessity is for the actor to maintain a precision of feeling and an architecture of response that allows him to swing through the line without falling into rant. To some extent this is a quality any actor must achieve in any passage of intense emotion, but here it is the dominant quality, the one on which the greatest demand is made. Different roles stress different demands. Again the comparison with Hamlet is helpful. The problem with the lines from *Hamlet* I quoted a few moments ago is that, by contrast with *Lear*, it is all too easy to make them superficially musical and thus to lose the play of distinctions and contrasts the words imply in the rapid, nicely modulated interplay of their sounds. Here as everywhere in the role of Hamlet, the challenge is to impose a meaningful coherence on materials that are various, changing, subtly differentiated, and quick moving. When Hamlet tells the players they must remain coherent even in the "very torrent, tempest, and (as I may say) whirlwind of your passion" (III, ii, 5-7), the actor must be at pains to do justice to this volley of interesting distinctions, with their mixture of playfulness, urgency, and critical reflection, while still holding the speech and the scene together and speaking it all trippingly on the tongue. As in *Lear*, the speaking of these passages is part of the fundamental action of the play.

The verse texture I have been talking about in *Lear* makes its greatest demands upon the actor when Lear confronts the storm in Act III:

> Blow, winds, and crack your cheeks. Rage, blow!
>
> (III, ii, 1)

These words are resistant. Each threatens to stop the line dead, to exhaust or baffle the actor's power to articulate. There is no easy musical way to link them. The consonants clash, the vowels expand. It is hard to move from "blow" to "winds" and to get up further energy for "crack your cheeks"; then there are two more imperatives to go, and that only completes the first line. For of course the speech continues:

Blow, winds, and crack your cheeks. Rage, blow!
You cataracts and hurricanoes, spout
Till you have drenched our steeples, drowned the cocks.
You sulph'rous and thought-executing fires,
Vaunt-couriers of oak-cleaving thunderbolts,
Singe my white head. And thou, all-shaking thunder,
Strike flat the thick rotundity o' th' world.

(1-7)

The actor's problem here is to maintain some movement of thought and articulation that will carry him through the dead stopping explosions of "rage" and "blow" and on to the other unwieldy, massively active words.

It should be noted, too, that the effort of speech required here echoes Lear's complex relation to the storm. Lear fights the storm, but he also uses it as a means of releasing his own feelings. He claims later that the tempest in his mind keeps him from noticing the tempest around him, but this is plainly inaccurate. For it is through Lear's dialogue with the storm that the audience becomes aware of the tempest in his mind, and it is by playing to the storm that Lear confronts his emotions.

In the speech I have just quoted, Lear is once more attempting to establish the connection between himself and the outside world he has desperately tried to maintain throughout the play. That is, under the stress of his own torment and shame, he again tries to thrust any source of emotional disturbance away from him by uttering angry commands. But now the emotion that is wracking him is so great that it can only be uttered, that is, projected outward, as a total destruction of nature, a cracking of nature's molds, and the effort required to project it outward is captured by the actor's effort to address the storm. The vocal effort needed to get from "blow" to "winds" and so on embodies this, for it is like trying to reach up and touch the storm, to become the thunder and the wind. The storm is significantly called "thought-executing," for in it we feel the explosive release of the thoughts Lear can no longer keep down.[4]

Lear's relation to the storm swings rapidly from commanding it to insulting it to holding his tongue again, and then he returns to identifying with the storm—but now no physical effort of emulation is involved. He is no longer acting out the storm but, as it were, imagining it. And he imagines it in terms of its effects on a population of hidden sinners:

> Tremble, thou wretch,
> That hast within thee undivulgèd crimes
> Unwhipped of justice. Hide thee, thou bloody hand,
> Thou perjured, and thou simular of virtue
> That art incestuous. Caitiff, to pieces shake,
> That under covert and convenient seeming
> Has practiced on man's life.
> (51-57)

Two points are interesting here. First, this is the first time in the play that Lear focusses on other individuals as centers of suffering. Second, Lear connects the active power of the storm with the eruption of hidden evil. The moral point here is less important than the psychological one. Lear suddenly is no longer talking about violence which comes from outside but about violence that bursts from within:

> Close pent-up guilts,
> Rive your concealing continents and cry
> These dreadful summoners grace.
> (57-59)

This shift to erupting guilt makes the lines that follow—"I am a man/More sinned against than sinning"—complex indeed. For Lear is moved to protest the injustice of his suffering, not, as one might expect, by thoughts of what he is being subjected to, but by thoughts of guilt bursting out. What he suffers seems bound up in his mind with guilt, guilt associated with sexual crimes and murder. Perhaps he experiences the force of his emotions as murderous and sexually irregular. The actor can find the emotional life that keeps this scene from degenerating into rant only by carefully charting how Lear's rapidly varying attack on the storm follows the surges of that inner suffering he now begins to acknowledge. He rives his own concealing continents to do so.

It is at this point that Lear says his wits are turning, and suddenly directs his attention to yet another center of suffering. This time it is a real person, not an imagined throng of sinners. He becomes aware that the Fool is cold, comforts him, and admits that he is cold himself. Out of this immense, chaotic explosion of long-denied emotion comes a moment of minute, concrete, ordinary feeling, a tenderness we have not seen before, based on an acknowledgment of shared pain:

> My wits begin to turn.
> Come on, my boy. How dost, my boy? Art cold?
> I am cold myself.
> (67-69)

These moments of awareness and tenderness become an important motif in the play as Lear directs his new capacity for close attention to the naked wretches in the storm, to Edgar and, later, to Gloucester and Cordelia.


# IV


All the various motifs of performance I have been discussing have in common a demand placed on the actor—and a concomitant opportunity given him—to apprehend concrete, sharply defined foci of pain. They require that the actor keep *renewing* his sensations, opening himself to a particularity of suffering. This of course is crucial to our experience of the play. The actor's renewal of sensation, by keeping the part alive, keeps our own sensitivity alive in the face of *King Lear*'s avalanche of pain.

The scene in Act IV during which Lear meets Gloucester and Edgar on the way to Dover is full of such histrionic opportunities for renewal. There are several things on Lear's mind here: sexual loathing, revenge, a hallucinatory, at times satirical, vision of court life and of himself as king, a fool-like insistence on unpleasant truths in his conversations with Gloucester, and at the same time a tenderness toward Gloucester's suffering. But in every case there is a marked movement of scrutiny—Lear presses forward to examine some detail in its full vividness of sensation. Lear focusses at different moments on, among other things, Gloucester's blinded eyes, a mouse, a wren, a small fly, a man accused of adultery, Gloucester's tears, and finally on the hooves of a troop of horses, shod with felt, pattering across the great stage of the Globe theater.

A few examples from this scene will show the histrionic imagery at work. At its beginning, Lear imagines himself as king. His hallucination projects a world whose dimensions are freely changing. The result is that Lear constantly seems to be on the scale of what he encounters, be it a mouse or a flying arrow or a troop of soldiers:

> That fellow handles his bow like a crow-keeper; draw
> me a clothier's yard. Look, look, a mouse! Peace, peace;
> this piece of toasted cheese will do't. There's my gauntlet;
> I'll prove it on a giant. Bring up the brown bills. O, well
> flown, bird! i' th' clout, i' th' clout: hewgh!   (IV, vi, 87-
> 92)

The mental movement here is in striking contrast to Lear's stance at the beginning of the play, where he insisted on control, on maintaining a scale through which he dominated. His reference to the bow may recall his great image of irresistible authority in the first scene ("The bow is bent and drawn; make from the shaft"), but now he follows the shaft into the target and mimes its whizzing sound. From the grand com-

mand to the thing commanded in an instant, from the straining
bow to the little mouse, this new lability is a measure of how
Lear has changed.

As the scene progresses, the sense of smell is emphasized,
competing with touch and sight for prominence. Sharply concrete references to smell and sexuality are mingled. The hand
that smells of mortality, the little gilded copulating fly, the
soiled horse, and above all the genitalia of women are on
Lear's mind, and he responds to them as if they sweated and
stank with a combination of sexual abandon and decay. Even
a description of virtue is charged with a grotesque prurience:

> Behold yond simp'ring dame,
> Whose face between her forks presages snow.
> (118-19)

The effect of the syntax is to displace a visual image of chastity
downward so sharply that it emerges as a grossly suggestive
image of sexual license, and leads Lear quickly to sensations
of burning and stench:

> But to the girdle do the gods inherit,
> Beneath is all the fiend's.
> There's hell, there's darkness, there is the sulphurous pit,
> burning, scalding, stench, consumption; fie, fie, fie! pah,
> pah!  (126-30)

Lear's agony is immense. He has not yet emerged from the
tempest in his mind, but now he is harrowed by vivid physical
sensations, which he links to emotional disturbance, again, as
in the third act, connecting them with sexual transgression.
The denial of emotion, the association of unmanageable feeling with humiliating taint is still strong. Now, as Gloucester
offers to kiss his hand, Lear imagines that Gloucester is squint-
ing, peering at him perhaps lecherously. At any rate he associates Gloucester with the emblem of blind Cupid, which
was sometimes hung as a sign above a brothel:

Dost thou squiny at me? No, do thy worst, blind Cupid;
I'll not love.   (136-38)

He rejects love. More important, Lear connects love with the idea of painful scrutiny and does this by means of images that carry the force of the sexual revulsion he feels welling up inside him.

At the end of the scene between them, Lear continues to swing from one tack to another, from imagining a spectacle of injustice, full of specific physical images, to a tender awareness of Gloucester weeping, to the vividly imagined tightness of his probably nonexistent boots, and back to Gloucester,

If thou wilt weep my fortunes, take my eyes.
I know thee well enough; thy name is Gloucester:
Thou must be patient; we came crying hither.
(176-78)

and thus to a sense of the entire career of human life as smelling, weeping, and playing the fool:

Thou know'st, the first time that we smell the air
We wawl and cry. . . .
We cry that we are come
To this great stage of fools.
(179-83)

Then suddenly he turns to revenge, but it too is conceived in terms of immediate sensation:

It were a delicate stratagem, to shoe
A troop of horse with felt. . . .
And when I have stol'n upon these son-in-laws,
Then, kill, kill, kill, kill, kill, kill!
(184-87)

This last line provides an example of another memorable feature of the play's verse—the accumulative pattern, the use of intensifying repetition, and it offers a final instance of how the action of the actor shapes the meaning of the play. For what is the histrionic problem set by lines like "kill, kill, kill, kill, kill, kill" and "Now, now, now, now" and "Never, never, never, never, never" and "Howl, howl, howl, howl"? In performance they act out a tension between the desire for absoluteness of response and the need for renewal, between the thrill of letting go, of crying out, and the labor of concentration, of finding a precise image for each exclamation in the series.[5] Such lines long to be only a cry, but they must have a content or they go dead: they threaten to escape, as every audience and every critic longs to escape, from the dreadful particularity of the play. They too demand, and make possible, that regular renewal of sensation crucial to the role.

## V

I want to shift perspective now and consider briefly a few of the ways in which Shakespeare locates the small acting patterns I have been talking about in what we experience as the larger world of the play. I will take as examples some features of Shakespeare's treatment of action and space.

In Shakespeare's tragedies we normally feel that the represented action (*praxis*, in my jargon) proceeds from the interplay of some more or less controlled and steadily maintained personal or political schemes, for example, Hamlet versus Claudius, or Macbeth versus those he first displaces and later is overthrown by. Now, though it is equally easy to discern in *King Lear* the movements of warring parties whose fortunes swing up and down and though there is, when one reflects on it, a surprising amount of intrigue, public and private, in the play (the secret conference, scheming, suspicion, and letter writing that have always formed the staple of the drama of intrigue), our *impression* of the action of *King Lear* is likely to be more chaotic. All the scheming is felt to take place on the edge of a much larger disturbance (Kent and a gentleman exchanging secrets in the storm, Regan and Goneril hurriedly conferring after the first scene as the court breaks up in confusion, Oswald carrying letters back and forth while the world goes mad).

At the same time, a major activity in the play is expulsion: Lear expelling Cordelia and Kent; Goneril and Regan forcing Lear out into the storm; Edmund forcing Edgar to run away; Cornwall throwing out the blinded Gloucester. Even assistance is most often seen, not as taking someone in, but as helping someone get away to an unspecified or temporary location. Thus, the intrigue in the play communicates itself to us as a set of fragile strands of intention winding across a large and threatening outdoor space.

For the sense of space in *King Lear* is unique in the Shakespeare canon. Instead of being presented with the usual two or at most three major locales, we are in great part urged to think of the stage as representing a place en route. And these scenes are unlike the en-route scenes of the histories or other plays that, like *Lear*, have battles in them, because in *Lear* they are felt to be not stages of access to a major location (Shrewsbury, Dunsinane), but rather pieces of a vast, unlocalized, transitional space, the large, exposed, generally inhospitable expanse of England. The largeness of Lear's England has been stressed in the early moments of the first scene, when Lear responds to Goneril and Regan's declarations of total love:

> Of all these bounds, even from this line to this,
> With shadowy forests, and with champains riched,
> With plenteous rivers, and wide-skirted meads,
> We make thee lady.
>      (I, i, 63-66)

But the greenness and richness of this world seem to vanish with Cordelia's refusal and Lear's curse; only the largeness remains. After the initial explosion in the great, ordered presence chamber, the indoors of the play becomes little more than a series of ad hoc auxiliary confines—a hovel, a lodging, an outbuilding, some convenient, borrowed room for torture. The rest is outdoors, on the way, dust-blown, wind-swept and bare, a space crisscrossed by the play's many frail and circuitous threads of intention: groups hurriedly quitting home, search parties, messengers, outlaws. We see letters moving about through curious and uncertain routes. Not only the messengers but the senders and recipients are on the move, and the letters are read not at leisure but under stress—in a storm, in the stocks, after a fight to the death. This sense of large, unorganized space and of errant, improvised movement through it is fundamental to the play, and helps locate Lear's recurrent focus upon minute particulars of sensation.

Here again we are made aware of precision of response by its contrast with undifferentiated hugeness. Lear's small gestures of scrutiny and physical contact stand out against the large, chaotic space of the play. And it is against the same background that we see one of the play's familiar sights—people supporting each other, one leading another by a hand or arm, two supporting one, one touching another. Edgar, Lear, and Gloucester seem to spend much of the play reeducating themselves in feeling through the exercise of touch, and this, too, adds to the impression of a fragile thread of feeling poised against the storm.

## VI

When Cordelia wakes Lear, he does not know whether or not he is alive. To see if he is, he pricks his skin with a pin. It is a basic test, whose meaning is central to the play. To be conscious is to be able to feel pain. Where there's life, there's hurt. Next Lear wants to know if Cordelia is real and human instead of a vision or an angel. He decides she is real when he notices her tears are wet. This tender concentration on the facts of pain takes on a special strength when we reach the play's final scene.

Lear's whole last sequence with Cordelia's body is a series of sharp focussings that insist on the unbearable distinction between life and death. Lear attends carefully to the looking glass, the feather, Cordelia's voice, her breath, her mouth. His eyes are not o' the best, but he makes an effort to scrutinize Kent's face. Then he asks someone to undo a button—at his own throat, I think—and turns back to stare at Cordelia's lips. His last words combine his three great modes of enactment—the giving of commands, intensification through repetition, scrutiny of particulars:

> Look on her. Look, her lips,
> Look there, look there.
> (V, iii, 312-13)

There is also in this gesture a subtle formal link to the beginning of the play, just as the exhausted triumvirate of Albany, Kent, and Edgar echoes Lear's original division of the kingdom. For as the first scene, with its talk of "all" and "nothing" on the part of Goneril, Regan, and Lear, presented us with towering absolutes, standards of affection and rejection that we knew to be false, as compared with the specificity, the sense of limit, in Cordelia's "no more nor less" (93), so the last scene confronts us with the difference between life and death in terms of tiny particular distinctions we know to be truly absolute.

When Gielgud entered in this scene with Cordelia in his arms, his voice suddenly rose on the last word of "Howl, howl, howl, howl," and became a howl itself, an animal wail.[6] He achieved here the kind of emotional renewal, the kind of continuing specificity, that lines of this type demand. He was taking advantage of the fact that the lines are at once a command and a cry. But they are unlike the commands Lear utters in the opening scenes because they *are* a cry, and because what they command is a sharing of feeling. Like so much in the play, they confront the performer, Lear's onstage audience, and the audience in the theater with the need to *keep* feeling just when we might well wish to stop, to distance ourselves from the pain. And my point in this essay has been that the role of Lear, as Shakespeare has written it, is designed to carry the audience forward into a deep exploration of its own relation to pain and to the problems of feeling and not feeling.

When Gloucester tells Lear that he has learned to see the world feelingly, Lear answers, "What, art mad?" (IV, vi, 150.) For his own madness is a struggle in which he comes to acknowledge his feelings and through them to make a connection with the world that brings him instants of shared love and moments of illumination he could have attained no other way. But the play's ending makes certain that we do not sentimentalize these moments, that we continue to experience the kind of openness to feeling Lear achieves as something desperately difficult, charged always with a weight of possible terror. For to see feelingly means to introduce an element of risk into every human exchange, the risk of being incapacitated, driven mad, destroyed by what one feels. It is to remind oneself that one is always vulnerable, because one is not everything. "They told me I was everything; 'tis a lie" Lear says (IV, vi, 104); and when Cordelia first tries to tell him that no one can be everything, his first reaction is to feel that she is nothing. But without that recognition of vulnerability, as the experience of the play reminds us, and as it must remind the actor who attempts the title role, without that constant focus on the dangerous human facts of feeling, we are nothing indeed.

# V. Speaking Evil: Language and Action in *Macbeth*

ONE OF THE THINGS our analysis of *King Lear* has indicated is that the distinctive verbal texture of a role should be a clue to distinctive actions on the part of the performer. In this essay I want to approach *Macbeth*—and particularly its power to involve us in the mental life of its hero—by looking closely at Macbeth's language and the kind of acting effort it requires.

To begin with a very noticeable stylistic feature, Macbeth's speeches, like those of Hamlet and Lear, frequently present the actor with series of words that are strikingly similar— words which may or may not be parallel in sense, but which are rendered insistently parallel by devices of style. Negotiating these sequences successfully is an important recurring action in the play. It is not too much to say that it forms part of the characterization of Macbeth, for it markedly determines the way his character must be received.

In *Macbeth*, the typical organization of parallel elements is very different from Hamlet's "Bloody, bawdy, . . . lecherous, treacherous, kindless villain!" or "Tempest, torrent, and whirlwind," or Lear's "Vengeance! Plague! Death! Confusion!" or "Howl, howl, howl, howl!" Let me start with a very familiar example:

> This supernatural soliciting
> Cannot be ill, cannot be good.
>
> (I, iii, 130-31)

What is the relation between *supernatural* and *soliciting*? First, the sound suggests a parallelism which the sense resists—and indeed the sound resists it too, even as it suggests it. The

congruence of the two words is as uneasy as it is emphatic—
since all the repeated elements—the s's, the l's, the n's and
t's, the swift polysyllables—are tangled by the *differentia*, the
new sounds and altered rhythm. It has the effect of a tongue-
twister. And the interplay of meanings suggested by the words
reinforces the impression of movement into a tangle, a disturbing density, as does the content of the whole speech. *So-
licit*, in its Elizabethan meanings, is a word of manifold suggestion, linking all kinds of persuasion—evil, neutral, and
good; rhetorical, sexual, sympathetic, and manipulative.[1]
*Supernatural* only heightens the sense of doubt and attraction
implicit in the word it modifies. And the speech—expressing
Macbeth's rapt, doubting, fascinated interest in the apparition
he has just seen—continues through a sequence of similar
entanglings. Balances are set up which are quickly undermined
by unassimilated residues of sound and sense, and this makes
the movement from word A to word A' (and sometimes A")
neither one of opposition nor simple accumulation, but of a
twisting and darkening, a thickening in which the speech thrusts
forward into little thickets of sound and into reflections which
don't allow the speculative movement to exit, ending literally
in a smothering negation:

> My thought, whose murder yet is but fantastical,
> Shakes so my single state of man,
> That function is smothered in surmise,
> And nothing is, but what is not.[2]
>                    (I, iii, 139-42)

We may note similar effects elsewhere, as in:

> If it were done when 'tis done, then 'twere well
> It were done quickly. If th'assassination
> Could trammel up the consequence, and catch,
> With his surcease, success . . .
>                    (I, vii, 1-4)

What is the relation between *assassination* and *consequence*,
between *surcease* and *success*? Both in sound and sense, they
smother each other. The speech moves quickly and nervously,

indeed jumpily, which probably dictates Shakespeare's choice of "jump" for "risk." But the jump here is miles from the swift movement of Othello's

> Like to the Pontic Sea
> Whose icy current and compulsive course
> Ne'er feels retiring ebb, but keeps due on
> To the Propontic and the Hellespont,
> Even so my bloody thoughts, with violent pace,
> Shall ne'er look back, ne'er ebb to humble love,
> Till that a capable and wide revenge
> Swallow them up.[3]
> (III, iii, 450-57)

In the speech just quoted, the relation of the similar parts allows us to feel word A progressing to A', to feel A' as the release, the resolution, say, of the chord struck by A. In Macbeth's speech, the jumper from A finds himself entangled in A'. *Success* becomes a tongue-twisting pun on *surcease*; we are explicitly invited to think of *assassination* as throwing a net around *consequence*, and indeed the effect is reinforced by *trammel* and *catch*, emphatically related to each other and to the paired words they link. We feel *assassination* and *consequence*, *surcease* and *success*, snatching at each other.

Such a movement into gathering thickness or darkness is of course often explicitly described by Macbeth:

> Light thickens, and the crow
> Makes wing to th' rooky wood.
> Good things of day begin to droop and drowse,
> Whiles night's black agents to their preys do rouse.
> (III, ii, 50-53)

> Now o'er the one half world
> Nature seems dead, and wicked dreams abuse
> The curtained sleep.
> (II, i, 49-51)

We are dealing now with the characteristic Macbeth-sound, a suggestion of darkness, a sad heaviness, which visits the tongue in slightly retarding fashion, a heaviness in the midst of lucidity, a heavy swiftness. Perhaps it is not fanciful, in this Scottish world, to hear in it something of a burr. But the important point is that the Macbeth-sound is not a coloration or a harmony, something properly to be described as fixed, but an action, the effect of a movement of speech which is a movement of the mind.

But we have yet to describe this action. What kind of movement is a movement through these words? What kind of action connects A and A', does justice to their meanings, and moves on down the paragraph? To begin with, let me provisionally characterize the verbal movement I have been describing as, in a phrase, a snatching into the thickness. I choose "thickness" not simply because of "Light thickens," but because it points to an underlying pattern of imagery which I think is of the greatest importance in *Macbeth*. This is the motif of the thickening of fluids. I have in mind, for example, the filling of the air with rain, fog, and smoke; Lady Macbeth's blood thickening; the brew in the witches' caldron growing thick and slab; light thickening to produce darkness; the sea turning red with blood. What is communicated is not, for example, the sense of blocked flow we get so frequently in *Troilus and Cressida*, but of a fluid medium becoming dense.

This motif is closely involved with the peculiar sense of evil that informs the play. I must spend a little time here on the way we experience evil in *Macbeth* because, in spite of much excellent modern criticism on the subject, certain distinctive features of the experience appear to have gone unremarked. I think that in shaping his play of treason in the aftermath of the Gunpowder Plot, Shakespeare had very strongly in mind the kind of moral horror we ourselves have felt in our own days of assassination. Indeed, even though it failed, the Gunpowder Plot seems to have shocked Shakespeare's contemporaries as no single act of political violence even in our time has done. To Englishmen in 1605, the barely averted disaster seemed nearly absolute. The conspirators had come within a day of blowing up the King, his heir, his family, and, as James himself described it, "The wholl Body of the State in generall.

... The whole Nobilitie, the whole Reverend Clergie, Bishops and most part of the good Preachers, the most part of the Knights and Gentrie ... the whole Judges of the land, with most of the Lawyers and the whole Clerkes."[4]

The image of that catastrophe—an explosive manifestation of evil, absolute and as if out of nowhere, the sense that value and order could be wiped out in an instant—contributed, I think, to the investigation of evil that Shakespeare felt compelled to make in *Macbeth*. And so he began his play with a terrible noise, followed instantly by a loathsome and, for the moment, incomprehensible apparition:

*Thunder and lightning. Enter three* WITCHES.

This effect, so clear and definite in the text, is strangely muted in most modern productions. But it is plain that Shakespeare wanted to begin with a bang; he wanted to shock his audience. He knew when to be coarse as well as fine, and *Macbeth* is meant as a noisy and frightening play. In production, I would have that first thunderclap burst, very loudly, while the lights are still up, plunging the theater into darkness and simultaneously revealing the witches in full cry. The first scene should rush past us before we can recover. We do not need time to get accustomed to the witches. They are not supposed to be intelligible but frightening, uncanny, obscure. Shakespeare gives them only a dozen short, riddling lines, which broadly evoke a thick and baleful atmosphere and contain but one clear piece of information—that all the sudden menace bursting over us is on its way to meet an as yet unknown person named Macbeth. The scene ends as quickly as it has begun, plunging toward more noise and another shocking sight:

*Alarum within. Enter ... a bleeding* CAPTAIN.
(I, ii, s.d.)

I do not mean to suggest that the sudden thunder and menace at the beginning of *Macbeth* is anything like a deliberate allusion to the Gunpowder Plot, but an English audience recently familiar with the Plot would have been especially sensitive to the moral and metaphysical overtones of the opening scenes. The Plot and its implications help to locate the kind of imaginative effect Shakespeare is aiming at here and throughout the play. The initial explosion will later be echoed in the sudden darkening of Macbeth's mind, the turning of his castle into Hell, and the corruption of Scotland.

The doctrine of Equivocation of course reinforced this sense of evil for Shakespeare's contemporaries, and I think the imagery of thickening fluids helps us to see the real force both of the violent stage effects and the well-known motif of equivocation.[5] The destruction at one fell swoop of the entire ruling order of England, apparently averted only at the last moment; the readiness of priests of God to swear to a lie *on principle*— such discoveries must have seemed to many Englishmen abruptly to open an abyss of evil possibility in the foundations of normal life. Evil, we are accustomed to say, appears in *Macbeth* equivocally—and this is undoubtedly true. But it is easy to miss Shakespeare's emphasis. The main point here is not that evil traffics in false appearances, or that it is a perverted or negative version of the good, though both these ideas are certainly present in the play. Nor is it even entirely accurate to say that evil in *Macbeth* is unnatural. Rather, evil appears to Macbeth as something immanent in normal and healthy nature, a foulness violently potent in what is fair, like particles in solution or suspension. Good things can convert precipitously to evil, as milk converts to gall, as the witches suddenly appear, as sleep fills with bad dreams. Indeed, sleep is presented in the play much as milk, blood, and the ceremonies of society are, as a healthful medium which can suddenly turn foul. Banquo's prayer just before Duncan's murder is crucial:

> Merciful powers,
> Restrain in me the cursèd thoughts that nature
> Gives way to in repose!
> (II, i, 7-9)

The witches' prophecies have perhaps affected his dreams as they have Macbeth's waking thoughts. For whatever reason, even the good Banquo is aware that evil—personal evil, evil within oneself—is never more than a wink or a wish away. This sense of evil is different from any which predominates in other Shakespearean tragedies. We experience evil in *Macbeth* not as a malign external presence, nor as a rottenness undermining all things, but as a sudden thickening of a natural atmosphere.

The characteristic action of Macbeth's speech is an attempt to clutch at the atmosphere he feels thickening around him— and within him. He tries to push into it, grasp it, stop its motion, wade through it, sometimes thrust out of it. He keeps registering the new entanglements, the smothering densities his horrible imaginings force upon him. The actor's speech in these passages must accomplish two things—both render the entanglement and attempt to press on through it. He must negotiate the way *soliciting* comments back on *supernatural*, try to get out of it with *cannot be ill*, only to be pulled back further in *cannot be good*.

I have said Macbeth tries to snatch into the thickness, but he does this with varying intentions and results. Sometimes the movement is a fascinated sinking, as when he yields to the suggestion of murder in I. iii; sometimes it is a brief pulling out, as in the same scene when he says:

If chance will have me king, why, chance may crown me.
(I, iii, 143)

Not much later than this in the play, Macbeth begins to deal with the thickness in yet another way, by wielding it, projecting the thickness he finds in his thoughts into nature and calling on nature to sustain the atmosphere he has created:

Stars, hide your fires . . .
(I, iv, 50)

        Thou sure and firm-set earth,
Hear not my steps, which way they walk, for fear
Thy very stones prate of my whereabout . . .
(II, i, 56-58)

Come, seeling night . . .
(III, ii, 46)

Macbeth is a brave soldier, an active physical man—but the most striking thing about him is his imagination. Here the term applies in its most literal sense—Macbeth possesses an image-making faculty of nightmarish power. We get, in this play, as full a portrait of the workings of a human mind as we do in *Hamlet*, but Macbeth has none of Hamlet's interest in analysis. He doesn't tend to think abstractly, and he doesn't *like* to think about his situation in any form. But he cannot help thinking about it in images. When he is about to commit a murder, the image of a bloody dagger comes up before him unbidden; it is so vivid he thinks it is real. He wishes it would go away, but it will not. This is not a supernatural apparition, but, as he calls it, a dagger of the mind—the product of his imagination.

What is particularly important is that Macbeth's imagination is a moral imagination. The images it registers most vividly have to do with the moral status of Macbeth's acts and desires. It is especially sensitive to evil, and it confronts Macbeth with vivid and terrible pictures that express the moral repulsiveness of what he is doing. As the play progresses, his typical response to his imaginings is to try to act, and to act instead of thinking and feeling. Macbeth, in fact, would much rather do something evil than imagine its moral meaning. But the more he acts, the more vividly he sees the moral horror.

Shakespeare gives the images that throng Macbeth's mind a powerful histrionic setting by having Macbeth use them both to explore and to discover his new emotions. In this, he behaves very much like an actor rehearsing a role. For *Macbeth* shows us a man not only betraying and murdering his king, but learning to perform the act, as an actor might. That is, he uncovers in himself what a modern actor might call his motivation. But this term, though natural enough, is misleading. For what the actor playing a murderer and traitor must discover is not some nuance of intention—not why Macbeth wants to kill Duncan—but rather, a convincing capacity for the act. He must discover what it is *like* to be able to commit such a crime, to have desires and proclivities and mental activity large enough to propel him into the act. And this is exactly what Macbeth, in the early scenes, discovers in himself.

Macbeth observes carefully and with surprise the psychic readjustments by which he becomes a criminal. His first soliloquy allows the actor to develop the capacity for Macbeth's grand passion—for murdering Duncan and for *intending* to murder Duncan—as part of his performance. And of course it involves us in this development and makes it part of the central material of the play. In this speech, Macbeth maps and explores his new mental topography:

> Why do I yield to that suggestion
> Whose horrid image doth unfix my hair
> And make my seated heart knock at my ribs
> Against the use of nature? Present fears
> Are less than horrible imaginings . . .
>
> (I, iii, 134-38)

The histrionic imagery here allows the actor to build up a complex state of mind step by step. Macbeth begins with an imagined picture and a reaction to it. He fights against, questions, and gradually becomes absorbed in this picture of himself doing murder, a picture which is both his and not his, ambiguously placed by his vocabulary neither quite inside him nor outside him—it is a "suggestion" (or, more obscurely, the image of a suggestion), to which he "yields." The image in his mind frightens him, and the actor is given specific terms in which to explore his fear: heart beating violently, scalp tingling, and that jumpy, up-and-down movement of breath and thought which L. C. Knights has aptly described as a "sickening see-saw."[6]

The process by which Macbeth explores the capacity for evil that has appeared, as if out of nowhere, in his mind may be traced to its full extent in the dagger speech. Again the actor is allowed to develop his feelings through a series of investigations and discoveries:

> Is this a dagger which I see before me,
> The handle toward my hand? Come, let me clutch thee.
> I have thee not, and yet I see thee still.
> Art thou not, fatal vision, sensible
> To feeling as to sight, or art thou but
> A dagger of the mind, a false creation . . . ?
>
> (II, i, 33-38)

Like the image of murder which springs to his mind when he hears that he is Thane of Cawdor, the dagger is something Macbeth examines with close attention to physical detail. And the process of exploration itself becomes a theme for startled discovery:

> I see thee yet, in form as palpable
> As this which now I draw.
> Thou marshal'st me the way that I was going.
>
> (40-42)

To confirm the reality of his "false creation," Macbeth draws his own dagger, and then, staring at the knife he holds, realizes what his exploration has led to. The vision has placed a weapon in his hand, drawn him a step further toward murder. The actor is still supported by the step-by-step exploratory method, but now it is moving him from feeling to action, a development which will be expanded in the next several lines.

Like the prophecies he has heard from the witches, the dagger strikes Macbeth as both a cunning trap and an extraordinary revelation—a kind of supernatural solicitation:

> Mine eyes are made the fools o'th'other senses,
> Or else worth all the rest.
>
> (44-45)

Now he begins to project the terrible instigation, the dagger in his mind, outward into the world around him. Once more he ambiguously defines the source of the image which obsesses

him. He locates his murderous "creation" not in his mind but
in a deceptively objectified future—the "business" he must
soon perform has created the vision:

> It is the bloody business which informs
> Thus to mine eyes.
> (48-49)

The phrase almost acknowledges—but also helps to obscure—
the mental origin of the dagger.

Next comes the decisive movement outside Macbeth's mind:

> Now o'er the one half world
> Nature seems dead, and wicked dreams abuse
> The curtained sleep; witchcraft celebrates
> Pale Hecate's offerings; and withered murder,
> Alarumed by his sentinel, the wolf,
> Whose howl's his watch, thus with his stealthy pace,
> With Tarquin's ravishing strides, towards his design
> Moves like a ghost.
> (49-56)

What is striking here is that, as Macbeth thrusts the thickness
in his thought out into nature, he converts it into yet another
image, which allows him to develop his murderous propen-
sities further. He transforms his passion into action first by
imagining a figure he calls "murder," and then by imitating
the very image he has projected. The bloody business now
informs all nature, and through it moves the figure of Murder,
whose movements Macbeth copies. The references to Murder's "pace" and "stride" lead naturally to Macbeth's own
steps:

> Thou sure and firm-set earth
> Hear not my steps, which way they walk, for fear
> Thy very stones prate of my whereabout,
> And take the present horror from the time,
> Which now suits with it.
> (56-60)

The psychological and mimetic process by which a man can become a murderer has been very thoroughly laid out, both for the actor and the audience.

At this point, the histrionic complexity of the speech can be felt in a single word:

> Whiles I threat, he lives.
>
> (60)

What process of articulation in the previous lines has allowed Macbeth to describe them as a *threat*? Surely it is a movement like the one just described, the projection of his murderous design outward into the world. He sees his speech as a step toward murder, a threat. And though he can now dismiss what he has just said as merely verbal ("Words to the heat of deeds too cold breath gives"), the speech has quite literally gotten him moving. Moreover, it has done so by transforming him into the image of murder he has projected. Macbeth has made his choice. He is now an embodiment of the very atmosphere of horror he has described.[7]

The interplay here between imagination and action is characteristic of the role. Projection—the forcing of material that horrifies him outward into the world—is Macbeth's basic method of defending himself against his thoughts. It is also his typical basis for action. Even his familiar habit of trying to "outrun" his imaginings by acting on them is a version of this mechanism. Macbeth goes out and makes a murder in order to stop thinking about one.

Politically, he operates in the same way. He governs as he speaks—that is, his method of dealing with the evil he discovers in himself is to recreate the world in its image. The Scotland that Macbeth creates, like the thick night he invokes or the meaningless universe he describes in Act V, is a product of the dagger in his mind. Scottish politics under Macbeth reflect all the treacherous ambiguities of his mental processes. When Macduff seeks out Malcolm to urge that he lead an army against the tyrant, he is staggered by Malcolm's suspicions and the elaborate deceits the exiled prince practices to test him. Macbeth is the cause, as Malcolm explains. Menaced by the tyrant's system of spies and *agents provocateurs*, even a virtuous leader must behave equivocally.

The scene between Malcolm and Macduff is pivotal in Macbeth's fortunes. As it begins, with Macduff vigorously urging bold action to save Scotland, we are likely to feel that here in England the power of Macbeth to project his horrible imaginings will not apply. Like Macduff, however, we are quickly disappointed by Malcolm's doubts and self-accusations. Then, slowly and painfully, our confidence is restored. Macduff guides our responses, and his passage through the scene is very carefully designed. When Malcolm finally confesses that his confession of vices was false, that his claim to be a liar was itself a lie ("my first false speaking"), the atmosphere of equivocation is momentarily too much for his auditor:

MALCOLM.  Why are you silent?
MACDUFF.  Such welcome and unwelcome things at once,
          'Tis hard to reconcile.
                    (IV, iii, 137-39)

Macduff's silence at this moment is balanced by his similar pause later in the scene, when he struggles to assimilate the news of his wife's death. There he is not bewildered by equivocation but overwhelmed by feeling, yet again part of his pain derives from the equivocal situation Macbeth has imposed on Scotland. For Macduff, too, has been forced to act equivocally. Fleeing Macbeth, he has left wife and children at home, unprotected—a fact that has seemed suspicious not only to Malcolm but to Lady Macduff herself. Macduff's second pause allows human feeling to assert and explore itself. He confronts his feelings in their full contradictory mixture of guilt, anger, grief, doubt, and faith, all of which streak through Macduff's speeches as he emerges from his silence but still holds back from action:

And I must be from thence! . . .
O hell-kite! All?

What, all my pretty chickens and their dam
At one fell swoop?
MALCOLM.                Dispute it like a man.
MACDUFF.                                I shall do so;
But I must also feel it as a man.
I cannot but remember such things were,
That were most precious to me. Did heaven look on,
And would not take their part? Sinful Macduff,
They were all struck for thee!
                    (212-25)

When Macduff finally says he is ready to fight, Malcolm responds as if to a signal that a new phase of the action is about to begin:

                                This tune goes manly.
Come, go we to the king. Our power is ready;
Our lack is nothing but our leave. Macbeth
Is ripe for shaking, and the pow'rs above
Put on their instruments. Receive what cheer you may.
The night is long that never finds the day.[8]
                    (235-40)

From this point to the end of the play, we are aware of Malcolm's army on the march and in no doubt as to its ultimate victory. In the rhythm of the play, then, it is as if Macduff's pause has finally turned the tide, freeing Scotland from the tyranny of Macbeth's mind. Macbeth, of course, who rushes to dispute things so as to avoid feeling them, remains that tyranny's prisoner to the end. From the time the witches appear to him, he lives in a false creation, governed by a "fatal vision" that is his own.

&

As we have seen, Macbeth's movement of mind often takes off from an image or idea that will not go away, that insists on persisting. His thoughts thicken round it—the horrid image

of the suggestion of murder, the air-drawn dagger, the fact
that Banquo lives, the memory of Banquo's ghost. He keeps
coming back to it, and his language allows the actor to feel
the persistent image thickening his thought, sometimes accompanied by the effort of his thought to rise out of the
thickness—

> It will have blood, they say: blood will have blood.
> Stones have been known to move and trees to speak;
> Augures and understood relations have
> By maggot-pies and choughs and rooks brought forth
> The secret'st man of blood. What is the night?
> 
> (III, iv, 122-26)

—until he makes the move that gets him for the moment
beyond the obstruction in his head, but leaves him, as it were,
coated, stained, and smeared by it.

Two other incidental features of the part help throw this
habitual action into relief. First, Macbeth in public speech
often negotiates groups of parallel words more firmly than in
private, establishing their relation as one of wit, which depends on and enforces moral clarity:

> Who can be wise, amazed, temp'rate and furious,
> Loyal and neutral, in a moment? No man . . .
> 
> (II, iii, 108-109)

The contrast between this passage and the murkier soliloquies
suggests that the action here is an effortful keeping apart of
polar opposites. They collapse and contaminate each other
when Macbeth is alone. Thus the characteristic combination
of movements in the more private passages: quick, forward,
out of the murk; slow, mesmerized, sinking deeper into it.

The second point has to do with what happens when Macbeth gets angry. All Shakespeare's tragic heroes, with the exception of Brutus, are given passages of explosive rage. It is
interesting that Macbeth's efforts in this line are very different
from the rest, as well as being relatively infrequent and not
so memorable. The reason, I think, is this. When Macbeth

rages we feel he is rising, very temporarily, from the more absorbing arena of his own thoughts. While he rages, we note again the habit he has, or that his mind has, of keeping a single image obsessively before him:

—The devil damn thee black, thou cream-faced loon!
    Where got'st thou that goose look?
—There is ten thousand—
—Geese, villain? . . .
    Go prick thy face and over-red thy fear,
    Thou lily-livered boy. What soldiers, patch?
    . . . What soldiers, whey-face?
                (V, iii, 11-17)

Even here, it is the obsessive image, the pallor of the messenger, which focusses his attention. More typically, he is quick to drop back into the inner arena:

    Accursèd be that tongue that tells me so,
    For it hath cowed my better part of man!
              (V, viii, 17-18)

Rage is a diversion, almost a relief; it is the horror in his own mind that absorbs him and spurs him into action.

All Macbeth's movements in, through, and against the thickening texture he apprehends represent his effort to adjust to the evil that has erupted inside his head. What he keeps doing, in one form or another, is poking around to find where the evil comes from, or, rather, wondering at and attempting to come to terms with its equivocal presence in himself. We may understand Shakespeare's concern here more fully if we note a curious motif that keeps cropping up in the various portions of Holinshed's *Chronicles of Scotland* which Shakespeare drew on for *Macbeth*. This is the motif of the ambiguous origin of promptings to murder. There is, for example, the story of King Natholocus, who in a time of civil strife sends a trusted friend to a witch to learn what fortune holds in store for him. The witch declares that Natholocus soon will be murdered, and by the hands of the very friend who is asking the question. This leaves the friend in some perplexity. He reflects that if he tells the king the truth, Natholocus may put him to death just to be on the safe side, while if he conceals the truth, he may be put to death for that. And so he solves the problem—by killing Natholocus. In another place we learn that certain noblemen who conspired with witches against King Duff, "Had been persuaded to be partakers with the other rebels, more through fraudulent counsell of diverse wicked persons, than of their owne accord." And we are later told that "Through the instigation of his wife," Donwald ordered the murder of King Duff, "though he abhorred the act greatlie in heart."[9]

What these passages have in common is the ambiguous instigation of evil, the feeling that the source of evil action is both inside and outside the mind that undertakes it. This of course is Macbeth's experience with the witches, the dagger, the voices in the night, the bell which "invites" him to kill Duncan and which he himself has ordered rung. The experience of the play puts us inside Macbeth's head as he finds himself wholly committed to deeds whose moral abhorrence he registers with the intensest sensitivity.[10]

I have certainly not meant to account for all Macbeth's actions in these pages, nor to describe his character entire. But I hope I have succeeded in suggesting that his play forces us not only to imagine evil but to imagine what it is like to *commit* evil. Through the actor who plays Macbeth, we learn to develop our own capacity for murder, we learn how to choose murder, we rehearse a crime. We learn, as the play enables the actor to learn, by developing, extending, projecting, our own imaginations. The mind of Macbeth is constructed so that, unlike most criminals, he keeps acutely imagining the horror of what he is doing even while he keeps on doing it. The actor constructs Macbeth's criminal capacity by a series of attacks on the thick and thickening atmosphere which seems, from the very beginning of the play, to fall upon him like a thunder-cloud, but seems equally to be rising from within. The movement of the play in performance should be a flight from horror into horror, always a little faster than we expect, a flight like Macbeth's own flight from and toward the horror in his mind. Macbeth can never escape the weight of that instigation in his head, and his language, properly performed, performed as Shakespeare has designed it to be performed, allows us to share his experience of an evil which he discovers unaccountably present, a sudden deposit, a condensation at once natural and unnatural, inside him. For this ultimately is what holds Macbeth rapt through the entire play: the fact that the evil he grapples with is *his*.

# VI. *Antony and Cleopatra*: Action as Imaginative Command

## I

MOST of Shakespeare's tragedies—*Romeo and Juliet* is perhaps the only arguable exception—are concerned, one way or another, with human greatness. Their heroes are larger than life and recognized as such by those around them. *Antony and Cleopatra*, however, differs from the rest of the tragedies in that it is centrally *about* greatness. The discussion of greatness is the activity to which the play's characters devote most of their time. In speech after speech, indeed scene after scene, they comment on each other's greatness—acknowledge it, praise it, measure it by various standards, are moved and changed by it, proclaim their own greatness, consider what greatness means. Love is also a subject of the play, of course. But the claim of the lovers—and even of their enemies—is that they are great lovers, no pair so famous, as Caesar says, and their language of love, particularly when quarreling and making up, is the language of fame, nobility, and superhuman comparison. They measure their passion against the scope and power of the universe and against all competitors, human, legendary, and divine. The competition knows no bounds, and there is no interest in second place, even in the hereafter.

Most critics of *Antony and Cleopatra* have recognized its concern with one aspect or another of greatness, but insufficient attention has been given to what the play conceives greatness to be. I would like to look into its definition of greatness not simply as an abstraction, but as a way of experiencing life, a sense of process that critically affects our sense of action. What I have called a definition of greatness might more accurately, if more awkwardly, be described as a concern with a certain kind of greatness and its way of acting upon the world. It seems to me to offer a clue to the play's dramatic unity and to some of the problems it presents for performers and critics—to the way Shakespeare moves his actors on the stage, to the kinds of action we are shown and not shown, and to the difficulties and rewards of the main parts.

In *Antony and Cleopatra*, greatness is primarily a command over other people's imaginations. It depends on what people think of you and what you think of yourself. At the lowest level, it is style, effective self-dramatization; at the highest, it is a means of overcoming time, death, and the world. It is registered in the behavior of audiences, and a concern for greatness is reflected in a concern for audiences. The audience for greatness in *Antony and Cleopatra* is multiple: it is, first, the small group of people on stage at any time; second, the entire known world to whom Antony and Cleopatra constantly play and which seems always to regard them with fascination; it is also a timeless, superhuman audience, the heroes of history and legend and the gods themselves; finally, it is the audience of posterity, of whom we in the theater are a part. The play is very much aware that we have heard of its heroes before coming to the theater; their greatness, their ability to command imagination through time, has helped to draw us. When Cleopatra decides to stage her death—and it is a carefully planned spectacle—the immediate cause she cites is the prospect of an inadequate theatrical representation of her life, which will not do her justice but boy her greatness in the posture of a whore. And when Antony contemplates life after death with Cleopatra, he says that together they will make the "ghosts gaze" at them:

> Dido and her Aeneas shall want troops,
> And all the haunt be ours.
>
> (IV, xiv, 53-54)

Once more, it is the ability to command other imaginations that sets the seal on their greatness. Very closely associated with it, in this passage and throughout the play, is the ability to go beyond natural limit and thus to take on the transforming power of imagination itself.

Greatness, as Antony and Cleopatra possess it, is seen not as an aspect of one's deeds, nor even, primarily, as the potential for specific actions, but as a kind of emanation radiating from the two lovers across the civilized world and down through history. Even our first reference to Antony is not to his courage, strength, or martial skill, but to his eyes, "That o'er the files and musters of the war/Have glowed like plated Mars" (I, i, 3-4). And this sense of greatness as a radiant attribute is felt in the spectacle with which we are immediately presented. The stage directions for the entrance that immediately follows read:

> *Flourish. Enter* ANTONY, CLEOPATRA, *her* LADIES, *the* TRAIN, *with* EUNUCHS *fanning her.*
>
> (I, i, 10 s.d.)

One of the effects here, of course, is to place Antony amid the court of Egypt. There are no other Romans with him, so Antony is merely part of the entourage, part of the spectacle of Cleopatra's power which will add weight to Philo's description of him as a strumpet's fool. But the court is presented to us in its characteristic activity of *tending* Cleopatra, and this activity will catch our eye in the theater. Antony, Philo has said, has become the bellows and the fan to cool a gypsy's lust, and we immediately see Eunuchs fanning Cleopatra. The spectacle of the court of Egypt actively tending Cleopatra occurs repeatedly in the text and is repeatedly referred to, most notably in Enobarbus' speech and in the preparations surrounding Cleopatra's death. And there are many natural opportunities for it which go unmarked in the stage directions. Very likely, it should happen whenever the Queen appears attended. It will certainly form part of the audience's enduring picture of Cleopatra. What can all this tending and fanning mean?

Enobarbus' speech, in its elaboration of the picture, offers a clue. First of all, as Enobarbus makes clear, the tending of Cleopatra is an activity which expresses and contributes to her greatness, especially in the sense of imaginative command. It does so by a battery of transformations—in which all the objects and persons that tend her pass beyond natural limit, and in which nature itself is transformed as if by a desire to worship Cleopatra. The barge is a throne and its perfume makes the winds lovesick; the water seems controlled by the flute music which establishes a rhythm for the silver oars; it seems amorous of their strokes. Next, we come to the tending and fanning proper:

> On each side her
> Stood pretty dimpled boys, like smiling Cupids,
> With divers-colored fans, whose wind did seem
> To glow the delicate cheeks which they did cool,
> And what they undid did. . . .
> Her gentlewomen, like the Nereides,
> So many mermaids, tended her i' th' eyes,
> And made their bends adornings.
> (II, ii, 203-10)

There is constant renewal here; every gesture of Cleopatra's attendants adds to her beauty, and they in turn seem to grow more beautiful in her presence. Her attendants seem like mythological creatures or works of art, but their superhuman loveliness is controlled, as everything in the speech is, by Cleopatra herself. Her nature goes beyond art:

> O'erpicturing that Venus where we see
> The fancy outwork nature.
> (202-203)

But if her nature goes beyond art, her art—as we have seen—commands nature. Cleopatra may beggar all description, but Enobarbus' powers of description have certainly been regally

expanded by his subject. The effect of the spectacle of Cleopatra attended in her barge is to command both nature and
imagination. She draws the city's people to her, commands
Antony himself, and the spectacle *we* see—three hard-bitten
campaigners chatting on an empty stage, one of them moved
to sudden eloquence, the others listening raptly, urging him
to go on—demonstrates how, even in Rome, she commands
Enorbarbus' imagination, too.

The constant renewal, the suggestion that the fanning both
relieves and excites, reflects a characteristic of Cleopatra herself, who makes hungry where most she satisfies. Summing it
up then, the spectacle of her appearances attended, with their
undulating movement, their splendor of dress, their warm
focus on Cleopatra, heightens our sense of the specific character of her greatness—its commanding, sun-like radiance, its
power to transform all it touches, its self-renewing fertility.
We should note, too, if we wish to possess the design of the
play, how the significances of this spectacle—not only as generally transforming, but transforming of Roman things—are
enriched for us over the whole course of the action. We first
see it, through Philo's eyes, as an example of a gypsy's lust—
the gaudy, self-indulgent world that has trapped and un-
manned Antony. That perspective is quickly challenged, however, and by the second act we see the spectacle from a different Roman point of view in the surprising relish and richness
of Enobarbus' report. At the end of the play, the tending and
adorning is part of the gallant, ecstatic preparation by Cleopatra and her maids for death, and it continues after she is
dead—again a transformation, but an enhancing one, of something Roman, the high Roman fashion of suicide.[1]

## II

Critics have occasionally complained that *Antony and Cleopatra* is actionless, but it is natural, given the play's notion of
greatness, that so much of its on-stage activity is taken up,
not with direct combat or intrigue, say, things we normally

would think of as action, but with spectacle, praise—and reports. The play takes unusual interest in reports, particularly reports about the great, and especially the imaginative impact of reports both on the reporter and his audience. We think, of course, of Enobarbus' report of Cleopatra. But there are also the play's many messengers and the reports that come to Caesar and Pompey early in the play. Caesar is moved to an impassioned apostrophe to the absent Antony as news of Pompey's strength mounts, and shortly afterward Pompey, having delivered a nicely parallel invocation of Cleopatra's charms, turns from jaunty confidence to apprehension and foreboding when he learns that Antony is on his way to Rome. These reactions help to keep Antony in our thoughts while he is off-stage, and, more importantly, measure his greatness by showing how thought of him dominates and controls the mood of others.

The most dramatically notable report, however, occurs in the fifth act. It helps to provide what little suspense and surprise the plot holds after Antony's death, a main line of intrigue leading up to Cleopatra's suicide. Since it may easily be missed in reading, let me take a moment to sketch its dramatic force. Shortly after Caesar has left the monument, Dolabella reappears, in haste, with news of Caesar's true intentions. His language to Cleopatra is very interesting:

> Madam, as thereto sworn, by your command
> (Which my love makes religion to obey)
> I tell you this.
> 
>> (V, ii, 198-200)

And he tells her, concluding:

>> I have performed
> Your pleasure, and my promise.
>> (203-204)

"As thereto sworn, by your command," he says, and "my promise." But what is he talking about? He has sworn to nothing; he has made no promise. No explicit order has been given. Nevertheless, something has commanded him.

On his previous appearance, Cleopatra has won Dolabella to her purposes, and the full extent of her conquest appears only here. But it is *how* she has won him that is of interest to us. She has succeeded by commanding his mood, impressing him with her greatness and the greatness of her grief. "Your loss is as yourself, great," he says. More specifically, she has won him by a report of Antony's greatness, an immense speech of praise which, even more than Enobarbus' report, has been a work of the imagination, an elaborate hyperbolic portrait, measuring Antony by the world and, finally, by the limits not only of nature but of imagination itself. It is couched in and carries to an extreme the play's language of praise for Antony:

> His legs bestrid the ocean: his reared arm
> Crested the world: his voice was propertied
> As all the tunèd spheres, and that to friends;
> But when he meant to quail and shake the orb,
> He was as rattling thunder. For his bounty,
> There was no winter in't: an autumn 'twas
> That grew the more by reaping. His delights
> Were dolphinlike, they showed his back above
> The element they lived in. In his livery
> Walked crowns and crownets: realms and islands were
> As plates dropped from his pocket.
>                     (V, ii, 82-92)

Cleopatra's praise of Antony as both equalling nature in superhuman power and going beyond associates Antony with imagination, and is in fact presented as a dream. At this point, Dolabella gently denies that there can have been such a man. But Cleopatra is ready for him. Antony is more than the stuff dreams are made on. He, too, is greater than any fancy that can outwork nature:

> But if there be nor ever were one such,
> It's past the size of dreaming; nature wants stuff

To vie strange forms with fancy, yet t' imagine
An Antony were nature's piece 'gainst fancy,
Condemning shadows quite.
                    (96-100)

It is Cleopatra's portrait of Antony that converts her audience.
Again, it is no anecdote of what Antony has said or done, but
simply a fantastic projection of his greatness that controls the
action, transforming Dolabella from a ready tool of Caesar
into Cleopatra's devoted servant, a man who imagines he has
sworn an oath and made a promise.


### III


The play's emphasis on greatness as imaginative command
has a radical effect not only on its treatment of action but on
the acting it requires of its two heroes. The actors who play
Antony and Cleopatra have to convince us from the start that
they are great. They have to do this not by their actions—
much of the time they are allowed action that does not show
greatness but at best asserts it—but by their direct command
over our imagination. We must always be aware of Antony
and Cleopatra's greatness as a genuine issue. Without the
audience's immediate assent that this man, Antony, looks like
someone we feel willing, on faith, to measure by superhuman
comparisons, without this the play will be tedious, empty at
the center. It will be truly actionless, for whatever unifying
sense of movement we get from the play depends on our sense
that from these two lovers there springs a power that can
dominate memory, compel extravagant loyalty, and exact the
fascinated attention of the entire world.

We might compare other tragedies in which the heroes are
considered great according to one definition or another, but
in which they are given early opportunities to exhibit that
greatness in action. Othello illustrates his nobility, courage,
composure, authority, in the first act through conflict, by chal-

lenging Brabantio and Brabantio's men, by overcoming the doubts of his fellow Senators. But Antony and Cleopatra must establish themselves in an atmosphere that comments constantly upon their greatness yet does not test it in action.[2] If anything, what they do early in the play—and indeed throughout most of it—works against their greatness, or against the ordinary measures of greatness in their world. The drama comes from their giving to all things, even the worst, a touch of majesty, making vilest things "become" their greatness.

Consider the problems of an actor who must enter on the lines:

> You shall see in him
> The triple pillar of the world transformed
> Into a strumpet's fool.
> (I, i, 11-13)

The strumpet's fool might not be that hard to manage but the triple pillar of the world—who even as a strumpet's fool remains the triple pillar of the world! "Stand up, Mr. Jones, and try to look like the triple pillar of the world." It has the rawness, the unsupported nakedness of the initial awful moment in an actor's audition, which in most cases is the crucial moment—when you step out and the producer, not waiting to see you tap-dance or do your James Cagney imitation, says, "He'll do," or far more likely, "He won't do"—and doing, in fact, depends not on what you do but what you are, on something in you—that, as they say, you either have or you don't. It is raw presence that is wanted. And the play makes use of, draws its meanings out of, that raw appeal, the claim pure presence in an actor makes on an audience's minds and lives.

In the case of Antony, what the actor must have is the presence of the greatest man in the world. Caesar, by contrast, doesn't need it. If on his first entrance we discover that he looks unimposing, why that can fit into a characterization well enough. His greatness may lie in cunning, or policy, or self-discipline, or realism, or the material power behind him.

But the actor of Antony must radiate a magnetism that justifies the admiration he receives.

Shakespeare has written a part that will reward and exhibit this power in the actor who possesses it. When he embraces Cleopatra on their first appearance, the convincing ease with which he requires "On pain of punishment, the world to weet/ We stand up peerless" (I, i, 39-40) gives an exciting resonance to their passion, which is essential to the play and which depends on our belief that this is a man who can make the world take notice by sheer charisma. When he makes his followers weep, we watch him deliberately using it. When in the third or fourth act he pulls back repeatedly from dejection, we respond to the radiance that returns.

Antony's dejection is worth further consideration here, because it helps us understand the distinctive accomplishment required of both the play's leading actors. It points not only to a side of Antony's character, but to the essential quality of his relation with Cleopatra. Antony's dejection is deep, and any production will fail that fails to stress it. It consists in his feeling that his greatness has been demolished. The land, he says, is ashamed to bear him. When he can feel a way back to asserting his imaginative command, his spirits invariably revive. Sometimes he fumbles about in his effort to reassert his greatness, as in the pathetic messages to Caesar, but he is utterly renewed even by winning a skirmish we know to be meaningless—not because he expects to win back his material power, but because his greatness is shining forth once more on all around him.

The revival of his spirits at his deepest moments of dejection depends, of course, on Cleopatra. The actor and actress who play Antony and Cleopatra not only must exercise a convincing magnetism, they must convincingly respond to its presence in each other. I know of no comparable investigation, before the nineteenth century, of the way two people in love act upon and change each other, and we must be sure to get the dynamic of their relation right. Now, some critics have taken "the expense of spirit in a waste of shame" as the emblem of Antony and Cleopatra's connection, and seen it as an example of a lust that periodically gives way to remorse.[3] This constitutes, in fact, a fair statement of the typical Roman view of sex in the play, and Antony himself seems to have it in mind early on when he says:

> The present pleasure,
> By revolution low'ring, does become
> The opposite of itself.
> (I, ii, 125-27)

But this is not what happens between Antony and Cleopatra.

Instead of attraction giving way to disgust, we find that whenever Antony reaches a peak of self-revulsion and anger at Cleopatra (never the result of sexual fulfillment, by the way), it is her sexual appeal, even, presumably, from beyond the grave, that enables him to recover. Significantly, the position he comes round to as a result is always one we recognize as more noble than the one he has taken in disgust, more appealing, more in keeping with that great property which should be Antony's. After Actium, after the whipping of Thidias, after the final defeat, Cleopatra brings Antony back from a moment in which he feels his greatness is gone to one in which we—and his audiences on stage—feel that he is exercising it again, whether it be in revelry, battle, or suicide. After he vents his wrath on her, she wins him back to her and to himself. Their mutual attraction, their sexually charged admiration for each other, though it drives them to folly and defeat, likewise stirs them both to greatness—to renewed vitality, indifference to material fortune, and splendid self-presentation.

The sexual magnetism which Antony and Cleopatra exert on each other is very similar to the magnetism of great leaders and great actors, perhaps indistinguishable from it. What binds Cleopatra and Antony sexually is not unlike what binds the world to them and binds us to the attractive presences of the actor and actress who impersonate them. The power of presence in an actor is perilously close to glamor, but it can be taken beyond the limits of glamor by art. This is what the actors of Antony and Cleopatra are required to do, and the process works as a metaphor for the type of problematic splendor their characters manifest. For Antony and Cleopatra are most actor-like in that they exhibit a magnetism that is culturally suspect. Paramount among the vile things they make becoming to the audience are the particular vices of glamorous actors. Cheapness and self-indulgence, narcissism and whoredom, hover about all their gestures.

The challenge here is to skate as close to shoddiness, to the disreputable side of glamor, as possible, to invite demeaning comparisons, both as characters and actors. Antony strikes poses, tries to make his followers weep, takes out his frustrations on the powerless. Cleopatra bitches and camps. Yet they never entirely lose their hold on their on-stage audience, nor should they on us. Shakespeare frequently invites us to judge them harshly, but any interesting performance of the play must keep the higher valuation always before us at least as a possibility, the sense that we are in the presence of some remarkable kind of human richness. They must be, as the text demands, showy, self-regarding, manipulative, concerned with "image"—all the familiar trappings of the glamorous "star." But while showing the seams of their talent, all the glitz of their art, they must show its irresistible power too.[4]

## IV

Once we think of the action of *Antony and Cleopatra* as flowing from the glitzy/charismatic presences of the leading actors, we become aware of a larger process that is everywhere at work in the play. To describe it in the most general terms, it is the process by which things that are attractive but of questionable substance or significance exert a transforming force on the apparently more substantial and valuable world. In so doing, they transform *themselves* into valuable and enduring entities. More concretely, the process is felt in the way

Antony and Cleopatra seem to make things happen by sheer magnetism, in the way Cleopatra can make defect perfection, in the way her art can transform nature and her nature outdo art, in the way imagination can alter and enhance reality.

An excellent way of appreciating the depth at which Shakespeare pursues this process is to look closely at one of the play's central terms, a word that occurs in some of its most familiar quotations:

> Vilest things
> Become themselves in her.
> (II, ii, 240-41)

> Fie, wrangling queen!
> Whom everything becomes.
> (I, i, 48-49)

"Become," in this sense of adornment or making attractive, occurs at least eleven times in the play, and is important not so much by virtue of its relative frequency as by the poetic effects to which it contributes. Shakespeare uses it to produce odd knots of meaning, where the general sense or emotion is more or less clear but an additional bend of suggestion is felt.

Let me give some examples:

> But, sir, forgive me,
> Since my becomings kill me when they do not
> Eye well to you.
> (I, iii, 95-97)

or

> Vilest things
> Become themselves in her, that the holy priests
> Bless her when she is riggish.
> (II, ii, 240-42)

At such moments we may be uncertain as to what is becoming to what or feel that the expected verb-object sequence has been suppressed or reversed. We would expect, for example, that attributes would become their possessors, as in *Mourning*

124

*Becomes Electra*, but in some passages we feel that the relation has perhaps been altered and in others we are specifically told that the relation is reversed, that the possessors become their attributes. "Observe how Antony becomes his flaw," Caesar says, (III, xii, 34), and Cleopatra remarks:

> Look, prithee, Charmian,
> How this Herculean Roman does become
> The carriage of his chafe.
> (I,iii, 83-85)

This last quotation illustrates, in very few words, the complexities the use of *becoming* introduces, and, more importantly, the response to life it stands for. The general sense, I suppose, is: behold how attractively Antony carries his anger. But the words *say* the opposite. The chafe makes the carriage, and Antony adorns it. The same process is at work in Antony's exclamation, "How every passion strives, in thee, to make itself fair and admired." It is not that someone's management of an unpleasant emotion is attractive. In both cases, the vile thing transforms itself into attractiveness.

Here we see a further complexity. There is, of course, another meaning to *become*—to turn or change into, to develop. The word is used several times in this second sense in *Antony and Cleopatra*, but, more importantly, whenever it is used in the first sense it also takes on suggestions of the second. A sense of transformation always flickers around its edges. *Vilest things become themselves*: the overwhelming primary meaning is that *vile things seem attractive*, but how easy it would be to say *vile things become attractive*. And the additional complication of the passage, the problem of how something can become *itself*, adds to our sense of development, of becoming as contrasted to being. More strongly still, the context of the passage firmly establishes the sense of continuing process, improvement, endless renewal:

> Age cannot wither her, nor custom stale
> Her infinite variety: other women cloy
> The appetites they feed, but she makes hungry

Where most she satisfies; for vilest things
Become themselves in her.
(II, ii, 237-41)

At this point we can conveniently relate these verbal effects
to the action of the play. What *becomes* of Antony and Cleopatra flows from their *becomingness*. We feel their attractiveness not only as a source of static pleasure but as a transforming force, changing lives, shaping the course of history,
making things happen in the theater. It is through their char-
ismatic appeal that Antony and Cleopatra act on each other
and on their audiences. They act on and act out their becomingness, striving even in death to *become themselves*, in both
senses of the phrase. Their becomings kill them, as Cleopatra
says, but they eye well to us.

One of the play's great emblems of transformation, of insubstantial attractiveness making substantial change, is to be
found in the speech Antony delivers in his last moment of
dejection. It operates in two ways: first, by suggesting Antony's
transforming power over imagination even while claiming he
has lost command; second, by a description of natural objects
that are at once evanescent and solid, lacking in substance yet
powerfully generative of significance:

Sometime we see a cloud that's dragonish,
A vapor sometime like a bear or lion,
A towered citadel, a pendant rock,
A forkèd mountain, or blue promontory
With trees upon't that nod unto the world
And mock our eyes with air. Thou hast seen these signs:
They are black vesper's pageants.
(IV, xiv, 2-8)

On the face of it, Antony is describing the insubstantial,
shifting texture of clouds. His point will be that he himself is
now of no more weight or account than they. But the feeling
of the passage runs quite contrary to its argument. Not weight-
lessness but solidity dominates our most immediate impres-

sion. The stately progress of examples suggests, not watery evanescence, but large, heavy entities, each definite and strong, and all with varying degrees of strangeness that have in common a quality of attacking and commanding power. The dragon's fire passes over into the fork of the mountain; the rock hangs pendent over us. Our sense of the clouds comes from the progression of objects. So does our sense of Antony's emotion and our emotion toward Antony. Each image is one which we can easily associate with him, with his authority, his elevation, his extraordinary capacity to fight, to rage, to brood, to inspire awe. We are not meant to feel an insubstantial Antony here, but a weighty one.

Each of us will likely differ in interpreting the individual details of this immense piece of language, and differ as well in isolating the source of its effect—but if we step back, as it were, to look at the whole passage again, we can agree that what Eros and the audience have before them at this moment is *what happens in the sky* and not its emptiness, not the insubstantiality of clouds but the sweep and scope of their transformations, a huge, strange, heavy, flowing process on the great stage of nature, nodding to the world like the trees on the blue promontory, as great as the world, for all the world to see.

Even at this low point for Antony, then, there is about him a vivid aura of imaginative command, perhaps even a shade of the old self-conscious artistry—he makes Eros weep. His imagery asserts the claims of the imagination even while reminding us of the traditional case against it. Clouds are a familiar symbol both for the imagination's vagaries and for its influence. Antony's description, while ostensibly giving a negative value to the clouds, actually awakens for us all the clouds' grand power over mood and the power of mood to spread and to infect other imaginations. Antony tells us that he is nothing, but he has not lost command over our thoughts. He rules them, like black vesper's pageants. His very loss of power is a great work of dramatic art, a pageant in which Nature and fancy outvie each other, to which we and Eros listen overwhelmed. Antony's speech is not only about his dejection but about the power of imagination to transform the world.

The passage is followed by another exercise of the imagination, a panicky lie, which has a transforming effect on the world of the play. Mardian, lying on Cleopatra's behalf, acts the part of Cleopatra dying, and this double bit of pretense finally prompts Antony to suicide. After the final defeat, then, the action is shaped by a series of deliberate manipulations of reality—deceptions (as of Antony here and Caesar later), self-dramatizations (as in the cloud speech and the conversion of Dolabella), and finally Cleopatra's carefully staged spectacle of suicide. The long concluding movement of the play, more than one-fifth its length, is dominated by this sequence of imaginative transformations, which accompany and bring about a corresponding emotional movement of enhancement—from meanness and agitation of spirit to generosity and peace, leading from Antony's rage through Cleopatra's panic, through the false report and the attempted suicide, through Antony's death in Cleopatra's arms, to Cleopatra's final sovereign moments.

## V

The process I have been describing—of imaginative transformation and enhancement, of making the insubstantial substantial, the questionable valuable—is very active in those final moments, and I want to approach them by way of an important and closely related pattern of imagery. A great deal has been made, critically, of what might be called horizontal oscillation in the play, its use of a back-and-forth movement in the alternation of scenes between Egypt and Rome, in the swings of Antony's emotions, and in many images—the vagabond flag upon the stream, for instance. And this has generally been interpreted as contributing either to a sense of ambivalence or of dissolution, or both. But there is another pattern of movement in language and action which is far more vividly impressed upon us, and which both controls and gives meaning to the horizontal. It might be called vertical, for contrast. The movement is both down and up, and the effect is one not of mere oscillation or breaking apart but of enrichment, renewal, and freedom. Put simply, it is a movement sometimes of descending into, but always of rising from, the generative slime, and it makes itself felt in the stage movement, the imagery, and the psychic action of the characters. But to put it simply is to run the risk of missing the fullness of its work upon us. For it is presented with great variety and suavity.

I want to stress the larger dramatic imagery here, but I would like to begin with one of the more frequently discussed verbal images as a way of making clearer the relation I perceive between the movements I am calling vertical and horizontal. When Caesar in a famous passage refers to the movement of the tide, he is not only indulging a typical bit of Roman political analysis, he is using imagery familiar to us from *Julius Caesar*, where it also stands for those currents politicians must study and follow:

> It hath been taught us from the primal state
> That he which is was wished until he were;
> And the ebbed man, ne'er loved till ne'er worth love,
> Comes deared by being lacked. This common body,
> Like to a vagabond flag upon the stream,
> Goes to and back, lackeying the varying tide,
> To rot itself with motion.
>                          (I, iv, 41-47)

The tide in the affairs of men goes this way and that in both plays, and he who does not seize it at the flood is drowned in it. And when Antony sees Octavia standing, as at that moment the whole Mediterranean world stands, between the two great competitors, he calls on a similar image, though gentler and more humanely felt:

> the swan's-down feather
> That stands upon the swell at the full of tide,
> And neither way inclines.
> (III, ii, 49-51)

But like many Roman judgments in the play this version of the tide image is not final. For tides do not move horizontally but, rather, vertically upon the varying shore of the world, and it is the vertical movement of the Nile from full to ebb— not aimless but fertilizing—that dominates the play.

The process by which the rise and fall of the tides is measured and used to sow the land is described at length by Antony for Caesar's benefit during their Bacchic feast, and runs through the play's imagery. *Antony and Cleopatra* begins with an accusation that Antony o'erflows the measure, but it is suffused with the suggestion that to o'erflow the measure is to moisten the earth and renew the world. Or, put another way, the tide of the affairs of men may be an endless oscillation, but the tides of nature endlessly create.

I hope this has given a useful notion of what I am calling vertical movement. In the play's stage imagery, it is most prominent when Antony is hoisted up to Cleopatra in the monument. I doubt whether one can overemphasize the force of this daring piece of stage mechanics. First of all we must pay full attention to Antony's condition. He has bungled his suicide, and we are meant to know that it hurts. For all his fortitude, he cries out in pain at least once. As early as *Romeo and Juliet*, Shakespeare had played the neat death off against the messy one, and here the messiness of the death, in which the hero must be seen as bungling, helpless, bleeding, in cruel pain, works against and with the wit, high language, and emblematic significance of his elevation. Up comes the dying Antony from the blood and mess to a final kiss, a final drink, a final cry of pain, and a final display of nobility. At the moment he reaches the balcony, Cleopatra explicitly strikes the note of renewal:

> Welcome, welcome! Die where thou hast lived,
> Quicken with kissing.[5]
>
>                 (IV, xv, 38-39)

Antony's movement here through and with what is low or messy to what is high and great is repeated more subtly but with equal theatrical force in the sequence of events leading up to and beyond Cleopatra's suicide. So much of importance is going on simultaneously in this last scene that it is difficult to talk about in any wholly perspicuous sequence. Perhaps it would be useful to begin by noting that there is more specific anticipation of the final death in this play than in any other Shakespearean tragedy. That is, there is more verbal reference to the particular circumstances in which Cleopatra will die. All the tragedies contain lines which may at least be construed as foreshadowing their end, and, not surprisingly, it is the love tragedies, *Romeo and Juliet* and *Othello*, that come closest to our play in this regard, with Romeo's dream, Othello's foreshadowing kiss, and his anticipation of chaos. But we have many more and more specific references to the nature and effect of Cleopatra's suicide—the serpent of old Nile, the breathless breathing forth of power, the am'rous pinches which are later echoed in the stroke of death like a lover's pinch, etc. I think Shakespeare may have been encouraged in this by the circumstance that this would be of all his plays the one in which the audience would be most familiar with the manner of the climactic death and most fascinated by it, and in which Cleopatra's way of dying would be one of the most famous things about this famous couple. For her death with the serpent at her breast was one way in which these lovers commanded imagination in posterity as they did in their lifetime. By anticipating it, Shakespeare is not only making capital out of his audience's state of mind, but he is using the fact of our state of mind as part of the stuff and meaning of his play.

Among the other sensations of the death scene, we are aware of ourselves savoring the fame of famous events.

In the deaths of both Antony and Cleopatra, we feel once more the force of the play's focus on greatness as imaginative command. Their deaths are insisted upon—by Shakespeare, by themselves, by the people around them—as imaginative acts that sustain and enhance their nobility, as ways of imposing their greatness permanently on the play's multiple audiences. It is not the fact that they die, or even that they die by their own hand. What matters is their style of doing it, how they conceive and describe it, how their audiences react.

Cleopatra's death is a superb piece of poetic transformation which quite insists on its poetry. Its best-known lines draw attention to their own verbal magic—their echoes, condensations, comparisons, ambiguities. The scene as a whole insists, too, on its power to change vilest things into lasting pleasures and great achievements, outreaching the Roman standard of suicide it seems based upon. Hers is no terse, stoic acceptance of a sword in the belly but a conversion of death into something gentle, regenerative, sovereign. Death is like sleep, sexual pursuit becomes a strong (and sleep-like) toil of grace; the snake is the worm that quickens Nilus' slime, a baby sleeping and feeding at the nurse's breast.

Like most of the ambiguities in the play, the treatment of the language here and the treatment of death itself works to take a relatively plain statement and promote it vertically, to invest it with greater attractiveness and value. Similarly, the events surrounding Cleopatra's suicide are arranged in a way that makes us aware of vertical promotion. Their sequence suggests a pattern of enhancement, a rising free from limit. We build up from Cleopatra as a helpless prisoner, whom we have seen struggling in the arms of her captors and kneeling to Caesar; through her scene with the Clown, with its puns and homely language, its basket and snake and talk of mud; through the play's final scene of tending and adorning, the putting on of the robe and the crown—a moment of stage spectacle that we see in the process of being created as well

as in its final visual splendor. Then, of course, she dies, having
become fire and air, with a great evocation of peace and gentleness.

The quality of sensation projected by the actress at the
moment of Cleopatra's death is one of the play's most concentrated expressions of the entire complex of feeling we have
been charting. As Lear dies in a moment of heightened perception,

> Look on her. Look, her lips,
> Look there, look there.
>         (V, iii, 312-13)

so Cleopatra dies in a moment of heightened sensation:

> As sweet as balm, as soft as air, as gentle . . .
>                 (V, ii, 311)

Lear focusses on Cordelia's lips, as his play has repeatedly
focussed on minute bodily particulars. Cleopatra dies in a
large, enveloping sensual experience, which has the enriching
ambiguity typical of the play. Is she describing, in these words,
the gentleness of the asp like a baby at her breast, or the stroke
of death like that of a lover, or is it her lover himself? For
her words finally gather into that name of names, so often
used simply as a superlative in the play, that infinite virtue
uncaught by the snares of the world, though tangled in them,
indeed adorned by them:

> As sweet as balm, as soft as air, as gentle—
> O, Antony!

## VI

Like Cleopatra's death, the play as a whole can be taken as
insisting on what poetry can do—and on the problematic
status of that power. To make vilest things becoming, to take
a gypsy's lust and, by fanning it, to convert it into a mes-

merizing radiance of fire and air—well, such procedures are a kind of trick, but they also echo some of our deepest experiences outside the theater, notably the experience of sexual passion and the related phenomena of human charisma. And if it is a trick, it is not a deception; Shakespeare, like Antony and Cleopatra, hides nothing. We see the moral questionableness of the material at every step, yet the enhancement mounts. The world of the entire play is bound to weet that its heroes stand up peerless—though no one can miss the point that they are of the earth, dungy. In them, as in poetry, every passion, however mean or ugly, can be made fair and admired—and we are left astonished that this can be so.

Are we left enlightened? One way of describing the elusiveness of *Antony and Cleopatra* is to say that of all Shakespeare's plays it is perhaps the hardest to accommodate to a notion of authorial intention. As a result, it is nearly impossible to discuss the play without making some statement about how we are to receive its peculiar mixture of glamor and demystification. I would like to approach this question by way of a flight of biographical fancy, which I hope will be taken less as an assertion of possible fact than as a metaphor, a step toward describing the kind of understanding the play communicates. I find it helpful to think of *Antony and Cleopatra* as written at a moment when Shakespeare, for whatever reason, had become particularly self-conscious about his own career. At forty-three or forty-four, he would have had a reasonably clear sense of his own greatness. Even if he shared his culture's relatively low estimate of the importance of playwriting, he must have been conscious of the unusual power of his mind. The intellectual effort required to produce *Hamlet, Troilus and Cressida, Measure for Measure, Othello, King Lear*, and *Macbeth* in half-a-dozen years would have struck even the most modest of men as extraordinary. Like any great artist he might have wondered what his powers could have achieved in a more practical sphere:

I turn away and shut the door and on the stair
Wonder how many times I could have proved my worth
In something that all others understand or share.

Antony, too, was admirably fitted for success in practical life—
and instead both he and Cleopatra had chosen to follow an
aesthetic path, the path of imagination and pleasure, had chosen to live out their mutual attraction—and attractiveness—
to the full. What value, what substance, could be found in
such a career?

And there was the other side of the coin to consider. What
was Shakespeare's responsibility for the moral impact of his
art? If, like Antony, he had followed his imagination where
it might lead, placing its promptings finally before the claims
of practical success, he had at the same time led a most public
life. Again like Antony (and like Cleopatra too), he had continually addressed the world in the most calculated terms,
attempting very deliberately to command its feelings. Like
Antony, he knew how to make his followers weep. Had he
done less harm than his heroes—or had he too corrupted
honest men?

> Did that play of mine send out
> Certain men the English shot?

Essex's friends had of course been idiotic to arrange for a
performance of *Richard II* on the eve of their rebellion, but
one could see their point. Whatever Shakespeare may have
intended, however orthodox the political "philosophy" of his
history plays, the power of his art made the possibility of
rebellion vivid, interesting, moving. In this, it loosened the
fibers of authority and moral restraint. And which of the
tragedies, with their immense indulgence of passion and fantasy, did not? Oh, they were perfectly correct on questions of
right and wrong. *Macbeth* deprecated regicide; *Othello* made
it clear one wasn't supposed to kill one's wife. But each was
a risky adventure in feeling and knowledge. Certainly it could

not be denied that imagination at its most importunate swept dangerously beyond moral lines. The power of language could make everything it touched precious, could, while the play lasted, make its own preciousness the center of value. In the figures of Antony and Cleopatra, Shakespeare may have recognized an appeal like that of supreme poetic fluency itself—the amoral splendor of the absolutely attractive.

In any literal sense, of course, such speculation is idle. We can never know Shakespeare's intentions, if he had any, and no intention can account for a work as great as *Antony and Cleopatra*. But the relation between poetry and the practical or moral life does give us a metaphor for our involvement with its heroes. As such it helps place the *showiness* of the play—its unparalleled emphasis on the quality of its own technique—and the similar showiness of Antony and Cleopatra. It also helps us in the difficult task of getting the play's ironies straight.

I do not think we are meant to "balance" the claims of Antony and Cleopatra with those of their critics; nor does one position dissolve or transcend the other. Rather, the main experience of the play is what I called vertical promotion. We are caught up in the process of enhancement. In the end, all the play's most questionable materials are transformed into elements of Cleopatra's final spectacle. They do not cease to be questionable, but the transformation sweeps us along. We accept it and enjoy it. At the same time, we are left with no confident way of locating or judging the process. Indeed—a further complication—we are left without a feeling of disturbance, with none of the moral vertigo, for example, that attends *Troilus and Cressida*. We are not allowed the comfort of knowing what we can "do" with the pleasure we feel; we are not even allowed the moral comfort of discomfort.

Shakespeare's position in all this may perhaps be glimpsed in the role of the messenger who brings Cleopatra the news of Antony's marriage to Octavia. What is his relation to these questionable lives he reports with such accuracy?

> O, that his fault should make a knave of thee,
> That art not what th'art sure of!
>                     (II, v, 102-103)

Though the poet is not, morally, to be confused with what he describes, still the good poet must be "sure" of the news he brings—and is thus in some sense implicated in it. Neither Aristotle's nor Sidney's excuses quite get him off the hook. Poetry makes nothing happen, says Auden, but he would have been more correct had he added—except for the things that happen when we read poetry. Poetry makes life seem very interesting, and, once aroused, there is no way to confine this interest to what is healthful, prudent, or community oriented. In *Antony and Cleopatra*, Shakespeare found a subject that richly indulged the ambiguity of the poet's position, a story that both challenged the claims of raw imaginative power and seductively breathed them forth. The play mounts no case against morality and public order; for certain instants, it simply leaves them behind.

The special theatrical quality of this experience can be felt in a question: what are we to make of a tragedy that finds its climax in an *easy way to die*? Like the acting it requires from its title characters, the action of *Antony and Cleopatra* puts a premium on sensual indulgence, on the unabashed exploitation of what is immediately attractive. Not for this play the suggestion that violent delights have violent ends, the idea which makes the action of *Romeo and Juliet* feel always like fire kissing powder. Instead we are drawn into the rhythm of indulgence itself, following out its becomings, seeking its own fulfillment, the sensual moment indefinitely prolonged, remembered, desired:

> There's not a minute of our lives should stretch
> Without some pleasure now.
>                     (I, i, 46-47)

> As sweet as balm, as soft as air, as gentle—
> O, Antony!
>                     (V, ii, 311-12)

We have seen how Cleopatra's last words focus on physical sensation. As an acting problem, that easy death must be made good by the actress' sensual conviction. Here, as throughout the play, we must be won over by the actors' ability to make the experience of sensation itself admirable and fulfilling—to demonstrate their commitment to pleasure in a way that makes an audience willing to entertain it as "the nobleness of life."

This special focus on the creation of pleasure as an end in itself—on sensuality in performance and *as* performance—places us in an unusual relation to the heroes of the play. Antony and Cleopatra are each other's best audience. They love each other, above all else, for the excellence of their performances ("Good now, play one scene/Of excellent dissembling") (I, iii, 78-79). If we may be said at all to identify with Antony and Cleopatra, it is their performances we identify with—with the ways in which they are most like the actors who play them, with their abnormal capacity to feel pleasure and desire and to transmit those feelings splendidly to the world. Our identification is the more breathless because we see them risking so much vulgarity and showing their bodies to be used and aging and greedy as well as attractive. We identify with their performances—rather than with the inner movement or constitution of their minds. There is nothing in Antony and Cleopatra that passes show. Indeed, the aim of their action is to find a show which passes everything—all obstacles and competitors—which shackles accidents and bolts up change.

Even more, perhaps, this is a play in which we identify with audiences, with Antony and Cleopatra as each other's audience, with ourselves as audience, and with the audience characters on stage. The play throws us into the position of Octavius in his tent, weeping at the death of a man we could not afford to tolerate among us, wondering (as we always wonder about Octavius) whether or not our tears are real. Our response to the play also resembles our response to and through Enobarbus, whose defection we regret, though in reason we cannot condemn it. As moral observers, we too would defect from Antony—yet to give up on Antony is to desert the life of the play. If we want to go on living after Enobarbus dies, we must remain loyal to this great corrupter of honest men, we must, as Cleopatra says, die where we have lived.

# VII. Characterizing Coriolanus

## I

ANY DISCUSSION of acting is inevitably a discussion of characterization, and studies of Shakespearean tragedy, whatever their approach, inevitably concern themselves with Shakespeare's characters and how we are meant to take them. Though we may feel, for example, that we know Antony or Cleopatra rather differently from the way we know Macbeth, nevertheless we do feel we know them. And when we discuss them, we find ourselves talking about their characters as we talk about people we know in real life—though most of us will adopt a stern tone from time to time and point out that there is a difference between character in real life and character in drama. In fact, there may be less difference, or at least a different difference, than we think—for on what, finally, do we base our confidence that real people *have* characters and that we are capable of describing them?

This is the trouble with characterization as a critical topic: we think we know what character is—or rather we think we know where it is and what kind of discourse best describes it. We think, or at least we generally speak as if we think, that it is to be found inside people, and we answer questions about character with summaries of inner qualities. This is a reasonable procedure and, it should be stressed, not a recent one. Nevertheless, it is true that in the past 150 years or so the description has tended more and more to stress the problematical and the psychological; character is seen as elusive, a subject for puzzle and argument, depending on the difficult and never entirely satisfactory attempt to chart the way someone's mind works. And debate about dramatic character is likely to turn on whether it is reasonable to expect this kind of novelistic presentation of character from plays, especially plays written before the nineteenth century.

It is at this point that the discussion of character in drama becomes dangerously tangled, through the operation of hidden assumptions. For the implication in the typical debate I have described is that the psychological discourse of novels and novelizing psychology is the most accurate form for describing character in what we helplessly refer to as real life. But does our experience of other people correspond more to the helpful summaries of a novel or to the un-narratized encounters of a play?

I do not mean to argue for any presumed metaphysical superiority of drama to the novel; what I wish to bring out is the potential for error in assuming that the original, as it were, of character is discursive and that drama must thus constitute a translation of that original into more foreign terms. It should be noted that my distinction applies not only to nineteeth-century novels and modern psychology, but to all discursive accounts of character, including Aristotle, Burton, or whom you will. By comparison with any mode of discursive analysis, it can at least be argued that our experience as members of a theater audience comes closer to the way in which we apprehend character in our daily encounters. Surely our efforts to characterize our friends and enemies—even the effort to characterize them *as* friends and enemies—follow, and always to a degree haltingly, after our experience of them, experience which, in the first instance, we approach through what Francis Fergusson calls the histrionic sensibility, the art, as it were, of finding the mind's construction in the face.

The notion of characterization as description may well have had a significant influence on the study of character in drama. I think it explains why, beginning with Aristotle, critics frequently maintain that character is somehow of secondary importance in drama, the implication clearly being that it is more important elsewhere, presumably in real life. With the conception of character, as with so much else, the hidden assumptions behind our normal critical vocabulary tend to make drama parasitic on narrative, and thus to distort our understanding of the effects and methods of the dramatist from the start.

I turn to these matters now, in my final chapter, because they are engaged with special clarity by *Coriolanus*. Shakespeare's last tragedy submits the whole question of character to a remarkable analysis. To begin with a point to which I would like to devote extended attention, it exhibits a concern unique in the Shakespearean canon with discursive characterization of the kind we recognize as distinctly modern and familiar—the nice and argumentative discrimination of psychological qualities. It contains many passages in which Coriolanus is discussed in this manner by other characters, and the effect of these characterizations is to strike the audience as increasingly inadequate to its own unfolding dramatic experience of the man.

In no other Shakespearean play do people analyze another character in the fashion they repeatedly employ in *Coriolanus*. I have in mind not disagreement or uncertainty over motivation, as in *Hamlet*, but perplexity over what we would call a character's psychological makeup. In Shakespeare we often feel the presence of such complexity, but his characters almost never comment on it. The type of question Othello raises about Iago at the end of his play—what makes him do such things?—is almost never explicitly addressed, and of course in *Othello* no answer is even hazarded, except the suggestion, immediately rejected, that Iago is a devil. Iago's own motive-hunting is just that, statements of particular reasons for enmity, rather than analysis of his mental constitution.

*Hamlet* is the play that seems most concerned with the subject, but even there one finds no clear-cut example. When Hamlet asserts that he has that within which passes show, he is referring to an inarticulable depth of feeling rather than some hidden aspect of his character. There is much concern with ambiguous givings out in the play, and it may well point to inner ambiguity, but no character explores the question explicitly. When Claudius says, "There's something in his soul/ O'er which his melancholy sits on brood" (III, i, 165-66), his language may suggest the elusiveness to description of a complex personality, but the explicit content is either that something is bothering Hamlet or that he is up to something which, like love or ambition, is capable of simple definition and explicable as the product of an external situation, for example his father's death and his mother's hasty marriage. Perhaps more could be made out of "Yet have I in me something dangerous" (V, i, 262), or "Pluck out the heart of my mystery" (III, ii, 373-74), but again these are matters, at most, of resonance and implication, not explicit statement. And the examples I have just cited are the closest we ever come in Shakespeare to the discussion of character as a complex and problematic psychological essence, with the exception of *Coriolanus*.

There the discussion begins with the opening scene. Like many of Shakespeare's tragedies, *Coriolanus* opens with the eruption of a dangerous force. The mob that rushes on stage carrying staves and clubs is meant to be felt as a threat; these "mutinous" citizens are on the verge of extreme violence. Yet suddenly, even before Menenius appears, the rebellion loses momentum. Within moments of their first appearance, the rebels pause—to discuss Coriolanus' character.

This is the issue the second citizen has on his mind at line 14, "One word, good citizens." He is answered in a well-known speech by a comrade who first says of Marcius that he is proud and, after an interruption, continues:

> Though soft-conscienced men can be content to say it was for his country, he did it to please his mother and to be partly proud ... (37-39)

The phrase has an air of simplicity and of caricature as well, caricature both of the subject and the speaker, but it is also very much a qualification of the speaker's original confident analysis. And the uneasiness of the formulation, "to be partly proud," which has provoked emendation and extensive commentary, suggests a difficulty in characterizing Coriolanus, even by an angry enemy who is none too scrupulous about his speech.

This kind of difficulty recurs at many moments in the play. Again, I am not talking about simple disagreement over Marcius' character, but about passages which have this habit of qualification, of instability, of attempts to specify a complex essence. The most striking example occurs in Aufidius' soliloquy at the end of Act IV:

> First he was
> A noble servant to them, but he could not
> Carry his honors even. Whether 'twas pride,
> Which out of daily fortune ever taints
> The happy man; whether defect of judgment,
> To fail in the disposing of those chances
> Which he was lord of; or whether nature,
> Not to be other than one thing, not moving
> From th' casque to th' cushion, but commanding peace
> Even with the same austerity and garb
> As he controlled the war; but one of these—
> As he hath spices of them all—not all,
> For I dare so far free him—made him feared,
> So hated, and so banished. But he has a merit
> To choke it in the utt'rance.
> (IV, vii, 35-49)

Aufidius first poses three reasons for Coriolanus' failure to "carry his honors even." This latter formula, with its obscure suggestion of a difficult balancing act, initiates a meditation that keeps sliding away from fixity and clarity of analysis. Aufidius presents his three explanations as if they were mutually exclusive, but they are not. "Pride" is the old accusation of the Tribunes, "defect of judgment" means perhaps political miscalculation or a deeper-seated inability to calculate shrewdly, and "nature," of course, can include the first two. But Aufidius quickly limits the application of nature to a specific failing:

> or whether nature,
> Not to be other than one thing, not moving
> From th' casque to th' cushion, but commanding peace
> Even with the same austerity and garb
> As he controlled the war . . .

Then, as if he felt that none of his reasons was quite sufficient, Aufidius goes on to complete his thought in a curious flurry of qualifications:

> but one of these—
> As he hath spices of them all—not all,
> For I dare so far free him—made him feared,
> So hated, and so banished.

It is the passage's sole point of certainty that most gives it a feeling of bewilderment. Why is Aufidius so sure that *but* one of these causes is responsible, "not all,/ For I dare so far free him"? There can be no logical reason; Aufidius simply feels that it would be too much to accuse Coriolanus of all three failings. Why? A sense of his character, of course, which underlies the entire speech and which Aufidius has been unable to articulate. And a further sense of it seems to rise at this very point, to comment on the difficulties Aufidius is finding:

> But he has a merit
> To choke it in the utt'rance.

This is another line that gives editors problems. The primary meaning, I think, is that Coriolanus' merit breaks in and chokes back the account of his faults, but the "it" is ambiguous; there is a clouding suggestion that his merits choke themselves. And of course Aufidius' own emotions seem to be registered in the verse. Coriolanus and his merits are certainly a bone in Aufidius' throat. The main effect is that the attempt to characterize becomes tangled and chokes on itself.

What has been evoked here, too, is the complexity and elusiveness of the very notion of character itself. The speech delicately catches the way innate predisposition, training, feeling, and choice come together and respond to external circumstance, the shifting changes of politics, and the feelings and actions of the public world—and also how, being a public as well as a private quality, one's character is modified, in a sense created, by the responses of other people, as Marcius' is by Aufidius. Coriolanus' character has something to do with the way other people choke on it. It exists somewhere between Coriolanus and his audience.

The paradoxical impact of Coriolanus on his society is felt strikingly in Aufidius' final speech:

> My rage is gone,
> And I am struck with sorrow. Take him up.
> ... Though in this city he
> Hath widowed and unchilded many a one,
> Which to this hour bewail the injury,
> Yet he shall have a noble memory.
> (V, vi, 145-52)

*Yet* is the important word. Though Marcius has done hateful things, nevertheless he will be loved. We have with Aufidius the sensation we have with so many of Shakespeare's tragic characters (though never with Coriolanus) that it is difficult to tell where play-acting leaves off and authentic feeling begins. Is Aufidius shifting gears for political reasons here? Or is he suddenly abashed? Is he asserting that Coriolanus manages, perplexingly, to be nobly remembered, or that he will see to it that Coriolanus is so remembered, in spite of his desert? All these notes mingle in the very believable compound of envy and awe that characterizes Aufidius whenever he contemplates his great rival.

This is not the only point in the play where the notion of Coriolanus' nobility is associated with perplexity about characterizing him. Many less elaborate passages have helped develop the idea. When the servingmen at Antium try to explain the mysterious quality they claim to have detected in the disguised Marcius, their language goes comically to pieces:

146

SECOND SERVINGMAN.   Nay, I knew by his face that there
was something in him; he had, sir, a kind of face,
methought—I cannot tell how to term it.
FIRST SERVINGMAN.   He had so, looking as it were—
would I were hanged, but I thought there was more
in him than I could think.
(IV, v, 159-64)

Of course this is a joke, whose point is that the servingmen
had noticed nothing, but this only refines the question of how
a noble character is constituted. The language of the servingmen calls attention to the "something" in Coriolanus over
which his friends and enemies quarrel. Even the play's repeated use of "thing" to describe Coriolanus suggests not only
his inhumanity, as is commonly argued, but the resistance of
his nature to characterization.

In the last act, Aufidius, on the verge of denouncing Coriolanus to the lords of Antium, offers to his fellow conspirators—apparently in all frankness—a further interpretation
of his character, which only adds to our sense of elusiveness:

I raised him, and I pawned
Mine honor for his truth; who being so heightened,
He watered his new plants with dews of flattery,
Seducing so my friends; and, to this end,
He bowed his nature, never known before
But to be rough, unswayable, and free.
(V, vi, 20-25)

Aufidius describes Coriolanus as having changed and become
politically manipulative. He has no reason to deceive his lis-
teners at this point, but his account does not square with the
Coriolanus we have seen, though we understand how Aufidius
may have arrived at it.

There is, moreover, a tendency in the play to keep before
us the whole issue of how we characterize people—whether
it be by internal attributes or external ones, by simple epithets
or puzzled formulas. The three scenes of Act II, for example,

have a very distinct parallel structure. This is the act in which Coriolanus, newly named, returns to Rome; and each scene begins with a prelude in which his character is debated by the people who await him. In Act II, Scene I, a conversation about Marcius between Menenius and the tribunes becomes a war of rather Overburyan character descriptions, Menenius topping the tribunes by offering two "characters," as he calls them, first of himself and then of his opponents. In the second scene of the act, the officers argue as to whether or not Coriolanus is proud and disdainful. Finally, the third scene begins with the citizens arguing over whether Coriolanus should have their voices; this prelude ends with words which sum up the aim of much of the play's dialogue, "Mark his behavior" (II, iii, 42-43). Heightening the parallelism, each scene ends with a conversation between Brutus and Sicinius in which they decide how to make political capital out of Coriolanus' impact on the people.

## II

What does this interesting emphasis on character mean? Surely it suggests that the character of Coriolanus is meant to be seen as problematic, and beyond this it raises the possibility that the idea of character itself may be under scrutiny—that the play may force us to confront the question of what a character is and how it is perceived. Here we must pause to examine further the peculiar relation of character and dramatic action.

Let me begin by returning to a point I raised in my introduction.[1] The fictitious person we watch on stage, Hamlet, or Hal, or Othello, is not an object, but a process. He is something we watch an actor making, not the result of making but the making itself. Hamlet, in performance, is not a tenth-century or sixteenth-century prince, not even a twentieth-century one; he is in no way physically separable from the actor who plays him. Yet we perceive him as a self, a character, rather than a series of physical actions. Where is that self? It is there, on the stage; it, too, is inseparable from the actor we are watching. Yet it is not the actor's everyday self, his biographical personality. It is something he is accomplishing by acting. A character, in a play, is something an actor *does*.

We are all too likely to think of an actor's characterization as an object, a presented mask, something produced and built up by the actor's preparation, as makeup or a dossier on the character might be. Such a product might well be described by a discursive summary. But a dramatic character is an action that goes on throughout the play.

It will be noticed that I have shifted to another meaning of the word "character"—that of imagined person in a drama. The two conceptions are linked. What is the character of a dramatic character? Clearly it, too, must spring from what the actor does. And what an actor does, first of all and ceaselessly, is perform. Dramatic character is inseparable from performance. Thus, as we have already had occasion to see, our view of dramatic character will gain by a consideration of the performance qualities built into the role, the necessary creative action of the actor called for by the script in order to project the part.

In the case of Coriolanus, certain problems of character have always been recognized, and they are illuminated by attention to some of the problems of performance. For the play, properly performed, gives us an impression of its hero rather different from that conveyed by a bare recital of his deeds or a discursive account of his language and behavior. We should start with the observation, particularly striking because of the great amount of discussion the character of Coriolanus receives in the play, that of all the mature tragedies this is the one whose hero seems simplest in inner constitution, a relatively narrow or immature self. Indeed, by virtue of the apparent ease with which he can be manipulated, he runs the risk of being interpreted as comic. Furthermore, many critics feel that the play's rhetoric is chill, and that this corresponds to something uninviting about both the play's ambiance and its hero—a lack of warmth or generosity.[2]

Now, though I do not think these comments give anything like a complete picture of the response a fully imagined performance of *Coriolanus* provides, there is a degree of truth in them, and they help define a major acting problem of the role. This might be described as finding what Coriolanus means when he refers to his own "truth" as something he is afraid of ceasing to "honor" (III, ii, 121). Is there more to this truth than doing what his mother wants, or fighting fearlessly, or hating compliments? That is, does the role suggest a freedom and depth of personality to which the audience can sympathetically respond? To keep Coriolanus from being simply comic means finding the passion hidden in the chill rhetoric, the richness of spirit beneath the many signs of poverty.

To indicate one or two ways in which the play addresses this central problem, I would like to draw attention to some qualities of performance that are required by the language of the role. Much of Coriolanus' language requires of the actor a kind of grip, a domination over complexity which is exactly the opposite of comic predictability. This grip depends on an emotional and intellectual penetration by means of which the actor maintains focus on a goal that is delayed and hidden by the movement of his speech. The histrionic action is rather like that of Coriolanus the warrior penetrating to the center of Corioles, thrusting ahead in battle, except that it cannot be rendered as a blind pushing forward; it is not like Macbeth's "Before my body/ I throw my warlike shield." It constitutes an important part of the action which is the character of Coriolanus.

The quality of performance I am describing is largely determined by syntax. A good example may be found in Act III:

> I say again,
> In soothing them, we nourish 'gainst our Senate

The cockle of rebellion, insolence, sedition,
Which we ourselves have ploughed for, sowed, and scattered,
By mingling them with us, the honored number,
Who lack not virtue, no, nor power, but that
Which they have given to beggars.

(III, i, 68-74)

If this sentence were diagrammed, one would see that it is the final pair of subordinate clauses—syntactically very subordinate indeed—which define its energy and direction. Coriolanus is primarily agitated by the idea that the patricians have given their power and virtue to beggars, and it is this which governs the notion of soothing them and is developed as sowing the seeds of rebellion. The actor must be gripped by this idea and render its presence in the speech articulate, even as he must suspend stating it till the very end. Thus the felt movement of the speech is not simply accumulative—this thing, that thing, and another—but a pursuit toward a syntactically buried point.

I think I can make this clearer by comparing another passage from Act III with a speech from *Othello*. This is Coriolanus' climactic outburst that goes from "You common cry of curs" to "I banish you." It is a swift and frightening forecast of revenge, but how different in its movement from Othello's

Like to the Pontic Sea,
Whose icy current and compulsive course
N'er feels retiring ebb, but keeps due on
To the Propontic and the Hellespont,
Even so my bloody thoughts, with violent pace,
Shall ne'er look back, ne'er ebb to humble love,
Till that a capable and wide revenge
Swallow them up.

(III, iii, 450-57)

The Othello actor must start out his passage with a desire for revenge large enough to be measured against the scope and

*151*

flow of the Pontic sea. But the movement of sweep and obstruction is grandly simple. The Coriolanus actor, by contrast, must struggle forward toward the instigating idea, *You corrupt my air*, which informs the three preceding lines of imagery and comparison, and which prepares the springboard for "I banish you":

> You common cry of curs, whose breath I hate
> As reek o' th' rotten fens, whose loves I prize
> As the dead carcasses of unburied men
> That do corrupt my air, I banish you.
>                              (III, iii, 121-24)

The intricacy here can be expressed another way. The opening lines of the passage appear to set up a neat symmetry: "whose breath I hate/ As reek o' th' rotten fens, whose loves I prize/ As the dead carcasses of unburied men," but the following phrase, "That do corrupt my air," unbalances this symmetry and, thus, to keep the passage alive there has to be an emotional thrust through the symmetries, which allows the crucial half-line to refer back to the earlier, "You common cry of curs." This problem occurs repeatedly in the role. A lot of the apparent coldness of Coriolanus' rhetoric resides in the balance and opposition he is constantly striking, but very often these balances get disturbed as the speech moves on, demanding a grip that keeps the balances clear and yet enlivens them by something not at all cool or settled.

A variation on this structure occurs when an apparently concluding phrase kicks off new images, requiring a supplementary charge of energy at a position normally felt to be subordinate or merely, as it were, passive:

> What would you have, you curs,
> That like nor peace nor war? The one affrights you,
> The other makes you proud.
>                              (I, i, 170-72)

Here, the subordinate "That like nor peace nor war" cannot be thrown away. The actor must pursue it with an articulation

which makes coherent the balanced opposition of "The one
... The other." And if we were to extend the analysis to his
whole great concerto-like first appearance, in which Marcius
enters at full tilt with what is in effect a long speech over and
against the interjections of the First Citizen and Menenius,
we would see how the larger structure echoes the tendency of
the smaller and in so doing prevents our first impression of
the hero from being comic. After all, what is it that keeps
Marcius, with his repeated "Hang 'em"s and "What's the
matter"s, from playing as a young Colonel Blimp? It is the
presence of a source of emotion which governs the entire
speech, pursued by Marcius through all kinds of syntactical
complications and shiftingly balanced reflections on the Roman populace, and which does not surface till the very end
of the sequence, when we learn that the people have been
given five tribunes, which Marcius correctly sees as a source
of future insurrection.

So, repeatedly, we have this construction, in which the delayed phrase may be modifier or object or even a piece of
information. But the effect is regularly that what is delayed
is a central source of energy, and we feel it radiating through
earlier phrases. Or, to put it more accurately, if even more
impressionistically, we feel its radiance being pursued by the
speaker down branching corridors which blaze and echo with
its force. The pursuit helps establish for us a great quality of
the hero—the quality of attacker. In the speeches I have described, the sense of attack comes from the pursuit of the
delayed idea, the buried trigger. If it were not buried, if the
speaker did not have to work fiercely to reach it, the pursuit
would not feel like attack, or at least not that magnificence
of attack we associate with Coriolanus.

In the great final outburst before he is murdered, the trigger
is the word "Boy":

> Cut me to pieces, Volsces, men and lads,
> Stain all your edges on me. "Boy"! False hound!
> If you have writ your annals true, 'tis there,

> That, like an eagle in a dovecote, I
> Fluttered your Volscians in Corioles.
> Alone I did it. "Boy"!
>                  (V, vi, 110-15)

The method I have been attempting to describe explains why that speech does not play simply as a confirmation of the Tribunes' and Aufidius' theory that Coriolanus is a manipulable figure: call him certain names and you've got him. Nor does it allow us to accept the explanation the play itself seems at times to put forward—that Coriolanus is, in fact, a boy of tears. The stimulus does not set off a mere raving reaction, but a pursuit, a kind of branching plunge, in which the whole being of the performer attacks the insult. Every phrase, "men and lads," "Cut me to pieces," "Alone I did it," "like an eagle," responds, separately, to "Boy!" Each bears *toward* the word, presses in on it, ranges pieces of a multiple attack that bursts into the clear only as the offending word is finally snapped in place.

Awareness of this technique will help us with at least one crucial passage which has often been misinterpreted:

> Though I go alone,
> Like to a lonely dragon, that his fen
> Makes feared and talked of more than seen . . .
>                  (IV, i, 29-31)

Most readings focus on the dragon, but the fen is the point. What makes Coriolanus most like a dragon is his isolation; indeed it is not even simply the fen that is at the center of the speech, but the power of fen-dwelling to make someone feared and talked of and hence lonely. It is not, then, a definition of his inhumanity Coriolanus gives us here, but of his felt distance from others. The dragonish qualities seem most to derive from being feared and talked of. They are, at least in part, an aspect of how society characterizes Coriolanus.

"Alone" is of course an important word in the play. But it varies greatly in meaning as Coriolanus pronounces it, and these variations are histrionic—that is, they represent differences in the way the actor projects a character through his performance of the word. In the passage just cited, "alone" suggests isolation, but it also is colored here, as elsewhere, by loneliness. By contrast, when Coriolanus turns on his accusers in the last act, crying, "Alone I did it," the word means "unaided, singling oneself out." This is mingled with an implied insult: "The Volsces can be beaten by one man," and a provocation: "I take full responsibility." It is a challenging statement of personal strength.

Now, there is another moment when the word is used in a very different sense, which is of the greatest importance for the performance of the role. And it is very different both in syntax and mood from any of the examples we have been considering. This occurs when Marcius addresses Cominius' troops after the successful assault on Corioles and before the battle with Aufidius. He asks for volunteers to follow him, and *"They all shout, and wave their swords; take him up in their arms, and cast up their caps."* At which point, he cries:

O me alone! Make you a sword of me?

(I, vi, 76)

This wonderful and startling line is not that of the isolated attacker, or the automaton, or the scorner of the crowd. It has a rush and surprised pleasure we hear nowhere else from Coriolanus. It is his happiest moment in the play.

Significantly, it is presented by Shakespeare as one of a series of stage images which intricately comment upon each other. It reverses the group of images we have had a few minutes earlier, first of Coriolanus scorning the soldiers as they flee, then deserted by them, then scorning them again as they pause to loot; and it will be partially reversed, restated dissonantly, one might say, a few minutes later when he angrily denounces the same crowd as it cheers him again. Finally, it will be most emphatically reversed in the assassination scene, the only other moment in the play when Marcius allows a group of men to touch him. But now in Act I he is elated, he accepts the praise and the physical contact of the crowd, and the word "alone" here means singled out by others, uniquely valued by people with whom he feels a bond. He is the sword of a courageous community—and the attacking hardness of the image of the sword (so often seized upon by critics as an emblem of Coriolanus' harsh character) is modified by the moment of joyous physical contact and celebration. This is the aloneness Coriolanus has felt himself bred up for, to be truly a limb of his country, a healthy limb of an heroic society; and for an instant his dream appears to come true.

## III

The shifting histrionic articulations of "alone" in the play are an index, then, of the full dimensions of Coriolanus as a dramatic character. We can, for example, appreciate some of the play's distance from its source in Plutarch if we compare the varying implications Shakespeare gives to "alone" with the idea of "solitariness," which Plutarch, in North's translation, borrows from Plato to describe Coriolanus. In Plutarch, solitariness is simply a vice, an inability to deal with others, the opposite of "affability."[3] Shakespeare's use of "alone," as we have seen, suggests not only a different and far more appealing character, but a far more complex notion of how character is to be understood. In the concluding portion of this essay, I would like to focus on how the idea of aloneness in the play illuminates two closely related themes. The first is Coriolanus' own conception of character—that is, not only what kind of person he wishes to be, but also how he understands character to be created and possessed. The second is the critique of this conception of character that emerges in the course of the drama. Taken together, I think they help us to understand more clearly the complex appeal of *Coriolanus* as a theatrical creation and perhaps something of Shakespeare's intention in writing the play.

We have seen that most of Shakespeare's tragic heroes entertain peculiar ideas about the relation of the self and its acts, ideas which poignantly reflect our own troubled sentiments on this bewildering subject. Coriolanus' version of this peculiarity is his notion that a man may be "author of himself." It is a phrase that evokes many of the same associations as his use of "alone," and it stimulates us especially because, while it plainly reflects his gravest folly, at the same time it seems fairly to express the very authority that makes Coriolanus so much more than a fool.

Perhaps no passage in the play has produced such troubled critical discussion of character as the scene in which he announces his decision to go over to the Volsces. His soliloquy seems in the most literal sense an attempt at self-authorship, at rewriting his play in the face of facts well known to the audience. Critics have frequently noted that it is an odd speech for what it fails to say, but it is, in fact, equally odd for what it says:

> Friends now fast sworn,
> ... shall within this hour,
> On a dissension of a doit, break out
> To bitterest enmity. So fellest foes,
> Whose passions and whose plots have broke their sleep
> To take the one the other, by some chance,
> Some trick not worth an egg, shall grow dear friends
> And interjoin their issues. So with me:
> My birthplace hate I, and my love's upon
> This enemy town.
>
> (IV, iv, 12-24)

For Coriolanus to describe his banishment, the hatred of the Tribunes, and the accusation of treachery as "a dissension of a doit" or "Some trick not worth an egg" is nearly incredible and suggests how far he has distanced himself from his feelings. The same may be felt in the overly neat conclusion, "So with me," and the flat and unconvincing assertiveness of:

> My birthplace hate I, and my love's upon
> This enemy town.

This distance from feeling is one of the perils of self-authorship. And in *Coriolanus*, as in *Lear* and *Macbeth*, the relation between feeling, action, and full humanity becomes very important. Certainly the moment of silence with Volumnia in Act V is reminiscent of Macduff's pause. It comes about because in Act IV Coriolanus, unlike Macduff, has failed to feel his banishment as a man. He has attempted to violate the natural relation between feeling and action, and like other Shakespearean heroes he must pay for it. If it is true that the defining problem for the actor in this play is to suggest an inner action deeper than the reflexive manipulable response seen by his enemies, it is interesting that Coriolanus' crisis comes when he tries to manipulate himself. To assert that one can do anything one wants is as humanly insufficient as to assert that one is completely predictable. Coriolanus declares, "I'll never/ Be such a gosling to obey instinct," but the creature who will acknowledge no obedience to instinct is as subhuman as the gosling.[4]

But even more than in one's relation to one's feelings, the fallacy of self-authorship may be felt in one's relation to the outside world. Like many of Shakespeare's heroes—Hamlet is the most famous example—Coriolanus must be tutored in the connections between theatricality and life, between the private individual and the social theater in which he plays his part and finds his audience. The lesson he learns, however, is unique to his play. If Hamlet must discover that a connection exists between play-acting and the heart of one's mystery, Coriolanus is forced to explore the relation between one's character and one's audience.

We can feel this even at the very beginning of the play. Most, if not all, Shakespearean heroes initially hold back from the opportunities for action that are first presented to them, and this is usually linked to a rejection of theater, though it is not always so plain as Hamlet's "I have that within which passes show," or so fearful as Macbeth's "Why do you dress me in borrowed robes?" At first glance, Coriolanus appears not to conform to this pattern, plunging with his opening words into a deliberately provocative denunciation of the crowd. But his opening line contains a refusal which precedes this eager engagement:

MENENIUS.   Hail, noble Marcius!
MARCIUS.   Thanks. What's the matter, you dissentious rogues . . .
(I, i, 165-66)

What is Coriolanus holding back from? I would describe it as the authority, the authorship, of an audience. Menenius offers him a name, praise, a characterization: "noble." It is a term Coriolanus values—in the last act, nobleness will be the quality he prays that the gods give his son. And the word "noble" occurs more frequently in *Coriolanus* than in any other Shakespeare play. But while he may readily pray to the gods for nobility, he will not consent to be called noble, even by Menenius.

In the same way, Coriolanus seems regularly to reject *our* interest in him. And this contributes to our perception of his character as cold or unsympathetic. The problems of his Act IV decision to revenge, for example—the "break" in characterization, the lack of transition, the flagrant inappropriateness of his remarks—constitute a defiance of the theater audience comparable to his regular defiance of his on-stage audience. Nevertheless he retains his power over both audiences—and it is clear that he *needs* them. Just as we feel an invitation to the audience in the actor's mastery of those syntactically difficult passages, or in "O, me alone!" or in the moment of silence, or the moment of assassination, or the physical release of battle—just as there are solicitations of sympathy here, enactments of aloneness which carry us along with the actor—so in his relation with the on-stage audience we see that the apparent defiance is far from complete. How else explain, for example, Coriolanus' repeated appeals to Aufidius to note how honorably he is behaving? As at Corioles, Coriolanus needs an audience to give him the name he has won. He cannot author himself alone.

159

This dependence of character on audience is echoed in the story of the benefactor whose name Coriolanus forgets:

> CORIOLANUS.  I sometime lay here in Corioles
> At a poor man's house; he used me kindly.
> He cried to me; I saw him prisoner.
> . . . I request you
> To give my poor host freedom. . . .
> LARTIUS.  Marcius, his name?
> CORIOLANUS.                                    By Jupiter, forgot!
>                                              (I, ix, 82-90)

The point is similar to the one Shakespeare makes in *Romeo and Juliet* about the way in which names, fate, and society are interwoven. The romantic attitude is that names do not matter; what one is counts. But our name reflects a real connection between our past, present, and future, between our selves, our acts, and our social being. Romeo *is* a Montague, and his name soon becomes that of the man who has murdered Tybalt. It matters quite as much as whether the name of the bird one hears is lark or nightingale. In the benefactor scene, Marcius has just become Coriolanus, a name which will permanently fix his relationship with Aufidius and help bring about his death, while his poor friend has become a nonperson because Coriolanus cannot remember his name.

Now, the relation between one's character and the behavior of audiences, especially as it affects the "name" one proposes to make for oneself, is of troublesome resonance to any great artist, and I imagine Shakespeare was aware of this. At any rate, he seems as he reaches the end of the great cycle of tragedies to become especially interested in the ironies of an artistic career. In *Anthony and Cleopatra* he tells the story of a man whose gifts have equipped him for the greatest success in the practical world and who instead casts his lot with a greatness that depends wholly on the imagination, on the splendors of gesture, passion, self-dramatization—an achievement as materially insubstantial as black vesper's pageants, and which the practical world will always associate with the arts of the gypsy and the whore. In *Coriolanus* he tells the story of another man whose ruling passion suggests the situation of the artist, a man who wishes to be the author of himself, an ambition, one would think, not only artist-like, but particularly theatrical—who but an actor can project a new self at will? Certainly it is an ambition easily associated with the appeal of high creativity. Who more than a great poet can make a claim to spiritual independence? Yet the theater is, of course, the most social of the arts. Indeed, it presents in its most unpalatable and least disguised form the fact that no artist is the author of himself, but a dependent part of an inconstant multitude, which is always in some sense interpreting him. Among playwright, actors, and audience, who is the belly, who the members?

There is, it should be noted, another side to the story of the poor benefactor with the forgotten name. For it also projects a vision of Coriolanus' fantasy of unconditioned power which is similar to the artist's fantasy of self-authorship. Perhaps one thinks that by being best warrior (or poet) one will gain absolute power over names—that one can command people by giving names or destroy them by forgetting them, that one can be free of the common cry, can stand outside of society, banish the world at will, that moving others one can be oneself as stone. This is an illusion, as any poet discovers, and as Marcius discovers when he tries to forget his own name and that of friend, mother, wife, and child.

ঽ

You will by now have grown tired of my saying, with Aufidius, "And yet." And yet I must say it again. For to end on the self-deluding aspect of Coriolanus' desire to stand alone would be to distort the play. The project of self-authorship, however mistaken, is bound up with the power and magnetism—indeed with the sympathetic appeal—of Coriolanus as a dramatic character. I think the issue here has to do with the nature of tragedy. In a sense all tragic heroes are authors of themselves.

I am certain that the writer of a tragedy feels more intensely than in any other form the struggle between what he wants to make happen and what his chief character wants to do. It is true of course that any tragedy exhibits a severe sense of scriptedness, but the play would be flat and tame if we did not feel that its hero had an equally exigent sense of the script *he* wants to write, of his own authorial power. Faced with some terrible contingency, the tragic hero makes it his own necessity.[5] Like a great actor, he makes the part he is given his own. And I think that when we argue over whether Coriolanus the character is cold and uninviting, when we ask whether his nature is fully expressed by the facts of his upbringing and the reflexes of his temper, we are asking whether he has the authority, the inspiriting freedom, of a tragic figure.

That is why the play must end with Aufidius' "Yet he shall have a noble memory." As with both Romeo and Juliet, and as with the self-authorizing ambitions of great poets, there is in Coriolanus something cherishable and indeed social about the lonely impulse which drives him. We return a last time to what I have called Coriolanus' truth. What did Shakespeare see in Plutarch's life of Coriolanus? He found there a great warrior firmly characterized as intemperately angry and hence given over to solitariness—for Plutarch, Coriolanus *was* a cold and uninviting figure—and he accepted almost everything about him except the characterization, which is to say he accepted everything except what mattered most to his play. Shakespeare seems to have looked at Plutarch's story of the choleric superman and said, "And yet." Here was a man whose whole life seemed to have been devoted to a notion of character; he was, in Menenius' Overburyan sense, the very character of a Roman warrior. And yet he could decide to betray Rome. And yet, being able to betray Rome, he again could give in fatally—more than fatally, embarrassingly—to his mother's plea. Shakespeare added complexities which show Coriolanus to be determined and manipulable in the most psychologically credible way—all that family history and revealing imagery. But he also added all the details which make him less easily characterized—his moments of unexpected response, the exciting complexity of his speeches, the range of meanings he gives to the notion of aloneness, and, always, that chorus of friends and enemies inadequately, perplexedly explaining him.

To sum it up, Shakespeare insists on the problematics of characterization in *Coriolanus* because he is there peculiarly concerned with a paradox: that the distinctive quality of an individual is at once incommunicably private and unavoidably social. As such, it is situated neither entirely within our grasp or the grasp of our fellows but, fascinatingly, between us— rather like the meaning of a poem or a play—between us in our encounters on the stage of the world.

Character lies in the interpretation of the time, as Aufidius puts it, and is thus susceptible to change and falsehood. And yet it is the most enduring thing about us. Perhaps this is what tragedy is about—that there is such a thing as human character. Perhaps it is only in tragedy that we feel that character as a personal possession really exists, in spite of the contradictions which surround it as a philosophical conception. For our sense of completion at the end of a tragedy seems to come not from any sense that the action could not have turned out otherwise, nor from our approval or disapproval of the chief character, nor even from the intensity of our identification with him, but from our sense that, through the action, the character has identified *himself*. Like the actor who plays him, the hero has exhaustively projected his unique genius, a process which can only be accomplished by acting in the world, before an audience, and exactly through those encounters which put most strain upon the defining qualities, the character, the actor is projecting.

All this may help explain why, in spite of much critical effort to the contrary, the idea of tragedy and the idea of character have remained persistently linked. More importantly, it suggests why the tendency to connect character and tragedy—and indeed to connect character and drama in general—seems to have survived what we think of as the particularly modern disassemblage of the concept of character. For our argument indicates that character in drama draws its strength exactly from the problematic status of character in ordinary life. Most important of all, though, at least from the point of view of this book, there is a further relevance. The notion of characterization that has emerged from our study of *Coriolanus* bears, not only upon the way all tragedies engage us, but on some distinctive qualities of Shakespearean tragedy, especially in relation to the idea of action.

First, it should be clear from the discussion of *Coriolanus* that "character" occupies the same region of conceptual space as "action." Like action, it is a radically unsatisfactory concept, and it reflects the same deep human need. To use the language of my opening chapters, it is a way of describing how being may be had, how inner events cohere and how they are connected to outer events. At bottom, the notion of character raises the same questions about self and act that we first encountered in *Hamlet*. Character implies a relation between inner and outer event. It identifies itself by movement out into the world from a private center of perception and intention, movement, that is, along the spectrum of action. Thus it rests on the assumption that such movement can take place, that motion across the bands of the spectrum exists and has a structure, an idea that *Hamlet* casts everywhere into doubt. Man is no more than a beast if he does not act, but every action is such as a man might play, and efforts to act significantly regularly lose the name of action. In the great third-act soliloquy, at a moment when Shakespeare has carefully led us to expect the most intimate revelation of Hamlet's character, we are confronted with an opaque abstractness of meditation that both in form and content calls all such revelation into question. We have seen that the difficulty and virtue of this speech lie in its demand that the actor, through his intensity of focus, project a highly specific core of individuality in its most personal relation to the possibilities of the spectrum. Yet he must act out this self in a manner that is virtually actionless, using language that is in large part almost evasively general, and in the very act of denying that the self can utter itself coherently in action. Here, in a particularly concentrated and demanding way, character is enacted by movement against powerful obstructions to even the possibility of such enactment.

But this merely reflects a larger Shakespearean pattern already familiar from these pages. We have seen that the Shakespearean tragic hero typically tries to impose on the world some more or less distorted and self-protective version of the relation between self and act. Like Hamlet, he may insist that his integrity exists independently of any actions that a man might play. Like Lear or Macbeth, he may imagine a monolithic unity of self and act, and strain to sweep so quickly along the spectrum that feeling cannot enter in. Or, like Antony, he may identify the nobleness of life with doing as he pleases. In one way or another, he attempts to be, in Coriolanus' phrase, the author of himself. And in every case the hero learns that he must abandon his confident sense of how the self is authored—how it establishes its authority—in favor of a more compromised relation.

This development constitutes an important part of the process by which the tragic hero attempts to take over the script that has been given him, to "make his part his own." He learns that he cannot do this by simple fiat, but only by the most difficultly adjusted engagement with the world around him. The Lear who says, "The bow is bent and drawn, make from the shaft," for example, resembles the later Lear who says, "We two alone shall sing like birds i' th' cage," in that in both instances he is setting up a relation of self to world that will allow him to impose his own necessity on the contingency thrust upon him. In Act One, he meets Cordelia's defection, Kent's disapproval, and his own agitation by presenting himself as an irresistible engine of authority. In Act Five, he invites Cordelia to a kind of endless visionary reenactment of their reunion as a safe refuge from further disappointment. Similarly, the Hamlet of both "Seems, madam? Nay, it is. I know not seems," and "The readiness is all," is taking over, actor-like, a difficult role and insisting on how he will play it in the face of severe threats to the integrity of his performance. But his first statement is a contemptuous refusal of contact with the world of appearances, the second an engaged acceptance of its scripts and uncertainties. In both plays the examples given chart a significant change of awareness. Both in *Hamlet* and *Lear*, the early quotation differs from the later in its much more confident estimate of how simple the process of authoring the self is likely to be, how easily and autonomously the private self can utter itself in the world of action.

One could go further and argue that the distinctive verbal texture of any Shakespearean tragedy is fundamentally linked to its hero's experience of the nature of action. The controlling imagery, the sense of "atmosphere" so richly present in each of the tragedies can be seen as expressing, above all else, the quality of readjustment the hero must make in his forced contemplation of the self/act relation. Thus, as we have seen, the spaciousness and order of the "Othello music" reflects the structure of personality Othello maintains, at first with ease but later only after an agonized recovery. The huge eclipses and frightful alterations which agitate the imagery of that play accompany the collapse of its hero's "perfect soul" and of his early confidence about the structure of his actions. Or, in *Macbeth*, the feeling of darkness and density, of equivocation and thickening fluids, helps draw us into the movement of the hero's mind as he explores the possibilities of evil he discovers inside/outside him, at once alien to him and yet deeply part of his being.

But if it is correct to say that, through the imagery of the play, we enter into the hero's developing intuitions about the nature of action, it is equally important to remember that we experience this through action and in the form of action. For what we are drawn into when we experience the "inner life" of a dramatic hero is not a static impression or formulation but an enactment. Performer-like, we enter into the actions that constitute a character. In *Macbeth*, as I have argued, we not only observe the hero's evil acts and learn how he feels about them, but we rehearse his capacity for doing evil, we possess the ground of Macbeth's evil action *as* an action which becomes our own. Through the actor, as we have frequently seen in these essays, we experience the possession of a self as an action, in which we participate. We *have* the hero's being because the doing of that being is passed on to us.

Perhaps it is no more than an inevitable bias produced by absorption in the critical method I have been elaborating in these essays, but it seems to me that this way of possessing a self through the mediation of an actor is absolutely central to the experience of tragedy. Indeed it strikes me that in arguing for the appeal of Coriolanus as a character I have been claiming not only that he has the freedom and depth of a tragic hero but, more specifically, that his play is capable of arousing in its audience a crucial type or element of tragic pleasure, one which has always proved difficult to explain, and which in fact can be accounted for only by reference to the actor-audience process. I am referring to the strong impression of positive accomplishment that we feel at the end of tragedy and particularly of Shakespearean tragedy. This feeling goes well beyond, say, the delight we presumably feel in safely witnessing horrible occurrences, or learning through vicarious suffering, or seeing even unpleasant things represented well. Surely it comes, at least in part, from the fact that we have actively participated in a most difficult achievement, the establishment of character against all that deprecates and derogates the coherence of the self. We experience a great expansion of power and knowledge in possessing, in action, an identity so definitively established. The communicability of character—as an internal imprint we can carry away with us from the theater, something which possesses us, in mind and body, as an actor's performance possesses us—this is the basic currency of all great drama. Shakespearean tragedy, however, gives it an extraordinary weight of meaning by forcing it to establish itself in the teeth of the most corrosive criticism of action and the self as satisfying concepts. Thus, in making my case for our involvement with Coriolanus, I have finally been insisting that his play engages us with its hero's character in a way fundamentally resembling all the plays studied in this volume. At the end of *Coriolanus*, I feel that strange response which a less apologetic age would simply call tragic exaltation. And if I have interpreted the significance of that mood correctly, it means we feel, in spite of everything, that there is in the end something about Coriolanus which is truly *his*, that it characterizes him, and that for us to have shared his character, by participating in it through the process of the actor's performance, has been an experience of irreplaceable value in our own drama of self-discovery.

To conclude in this fashion, by referring to an internal drama of self-discovery, is of course once more to introduce a term that puzzles philosophy, but this is exactly the point. For it returns us to the elusive, unshakeable grip that the idea of action exerts upon us. Certainly, it is not clear in what sense selves exist, let alone that we can discover them. They are, as we experience them in ordinary life, perhaps only spaces, outlined by a desire and movement that never leave us, unfillable and, as such, not to be had. But from these spaces our lives extend. Action is a notion that speaks to our need for such extension, however doubtful its sources, inconceivable its structure, and enigmatic its results. When we speak of self-discovery, we seem to refer to the sensation of having come upon something of our own, a self or part of one, that shimmers or presses at the source of action, that attempts to unfold itself into the world. In Shakespeare's theater we possess the selves of his tragic heroes, through the actors, as remarkably difficult and contagious unfoldings. By participating in their enactment, we touch the questionable shapes inside us, those hungry, ghostly outlines for which our language is at once so necessary and so inadequate. To have what we mean and need when we say we have a self, and to have it in commerce with the world in the way we mean and need when we say there is such a thing as action—this, I suspect, is a not inconsiderable source of pleasure in tragedy and very possibly its defining achievement.

# *Notes*

## CHAPTER I:   INTRODUCTION

1. *Hexis* from the Greek *echein* = to have, habit from Latin *habere*.
2. *Proceedings of the Aristotelian Society*, Suppl. Vol. XVII (1938). Readers who have difficulty with contemporary analytical philosophy are likely to find this still representative symposium a lucid introduction to the terrain. For more extended and technical treatment, one might start with A. R. White's anthology, *The Philosophy of Action* (London, 1968) and then consult such works as Arthur Danto, *Analytical Philosophy of Action* (Cambridge University Press, 1973), Donald Davidson, *Essays on Actions and Events* (Oxford University Press, 1980), or Jennifer Hornsby, *Actions* (London, 1980).
3. *Aristotle's Poetics* (New York, 1961), pp. 4, 8. This is Fergusson's gloss on Aristotle's conception of action; he takes the phrase from Dante.
4. This is not to be confused with the kinesthetic response I described earlier, by which we re-enact the actions of the play. I am talking about an action that is different from that of either the characters or the actors, a mental and emotional movement by which we attempt to follow or otherwise deal with what we see happening in the drama. Needless to say, both actors and characters exist for us only by virtue of the actions of our minds, but I am concerned here with the secondary process by which we try to order our initial perceptions of personality, incident, and performance.
5. The three terms appear as forms of *energeia*, or activity, in the *Nicomachean Ethics. Praxis*, often translated simply

as "action," refers to activities which aim, as we might say, at "doing" something, especially to other human beings. The aim of *poiesis*, by contrast, is to make or produce something; it is the action of craftsmen and artists. *Theoria* is mental action; its aim is to arrive at or understand some truth. Aristotle does not employ these distinctions in the *Poetics*, though there his *praxis*, the word he uses throughout for action, often seems to coincide with mine. For Aristotle, the creative action of the actor is scarcely an important part of the dramatic process, and he would certainly not use *theoria* in my sense of the term. Still, it should be remembered that, whatever efforts of creation may lie *behind* a play, the only artistic activity we directly and continuously experience when we watch one is that of the actors. Thus I choose *poiesis* to underline our awareness of the actor's ongoing process, his continual *making*, as a major component of the play's action. And *theoria* derives, like the Greek word for theater, *theatron*, from a common source, *theasthai*. Indeed the verbal form, *theorein*, with its suggestion of lively inspection and active attempt to understand, applies nicely to our action as members of a theater audience.

It should be borne in mind that my intention in using these terms is not, like Aristotle, to distinguish categories, but rather sources, of action. In particular, the common distinction between *praxis* and *theoria* as between action and thought does not apply here. Further reasons for this will appear in the discussion of thought and action in the chapters on *Hamlet* and *Othello*.

6. Princeton, 1972. For an extended discussion of *Hamlet*, See pp. 74-93.

## CHAPTER II: "TO BE OR NOT TO BE" AND THE SPECTRUM OF ACTION

1. J. L. Austin, "A Plea for Excuses," *Philosophical Papers* (Oxford, 1961), pp. 123-52.

2. For a discussion of the connection between rhetoric and plot in revenge drama, see my *The Actor's Freedom: Toward a Theory of Drama* (New York, 1975), pp. 97-100.

3. Rereading *The Idea of a Theater* (Princeton University Press, 1949), I find that Fergusson also speaks of a "spectrum of action" (p. 37). I expect I unconsciously borrowed the phrase from him. If so, it is but a small instance of my indebtedness to his great work. Fergusson means something quite different by the image than I do, however; his spectrum is an array of different kinds of action, while mine describes the linked components of a single action.

4. All Shakespearean citations are to *The Complete Signet Classic Shakespeare*, ed. Sylvan Barnet (New York, 1972).

5. Carol Carlisle, *Shakespeare from the Greenroom* (University of North Carolina Press, 1969), p. 102.

6. *Shakespeare and the Energies of Drama*, p. 88.

7. The importance of this awareness to Renaissance political thought is emphasized by Hannah Arendt in *The Human Condition* (Chicago, 1958). Indeed, though she nowhere refers to Shakespeare's play, two sections of her long chapter on "Action" seem of striking relevance to the view of action in history unfolded in *Hamlet*: section 25, "The Web of Relationships and the Enacted Stories," pp. 181-88, and section 32, "The Process Character of Action," pp. 230-36.

I use *vita activa* here in its traditional reference to political life (well summarized by Arendt on pp. 12-16) as opposed to the special definition she develops to extend its meaning to other activities.

8. There are a number of excellent studies of the speech as a literary construction. Harold Jenkins' long note in his Arden edition (London, 1982), pp. 484-90, provides a very sensible brief introduction to the criticism. For a specially sensitive examination of the speech's linguistic intricacies, see Stephen Booth, "On the Value of *Hamlet*," in *Reinterpretations of Elizabethan Drama*, ed. Norman Rabkin (Columbia University Press, 1969), pp. 164-71. Maurice Charney's perceptive comments on the use of infinitives in the

opening lines draw attention to a significant source of difficulty for the actor. (*Style in Hamlet* [Princeton University Press, 1969], pp. 301-302).

9. See, for example, Arthur Colby Sprague, *Shakespeare and the Actors: The Stage Business in His Plays (1660-1905)* (New York, 1944), pp. 150, 151; Gamini Salgado, *Eyewitnesses of Shakespeare: First Hand Accounts of Performances* (Sussex University Press, 1975), pp. 238-39; Furness' *New Variorum* edition (Philadelphia, 1877), II, 245-60, 270.

10. The way in which a variety of different performance attacks may still be gathered into a single "performance design" has been given extended scrutiny by Marvin Rosenberg. His most explicit discussion of the problem may be found in *The Masks of King Lear* (University of California Press, 1972), especially pp. 17-32.

11. For some of Shakespeare's earlier experiments in enlarging the range of performance of mental life on stage, see Daniel Seltzer, "Prince Hal and Tragic Style," *Shakespeare Survey*, 30 (1977), 13-27.

12. A reader unfamiliar with good acting—or, more accurately, with the difficulties of attempting to describe what good acting conveys—may ask, can an actor possibly suggest all this? The answer is, yes, easily, if he has the skill and desire to do it. Of course, to the extent that he is adequate to his task, he will achieve his effects with a seamless immediacy that quite contrasts with the laboriousness of critical analysis. My words are a necessarily awkward, slow-footed, and indeed incomplete representation of what can be condensed into a single performed phrase, given the notation that Shakespeare has supplied. The problem for the literary reader, even for one who is a regular theatergoer, may lie in his tendency to treat any moment of performance as semiotically exhaustible—the transmission of a finite number of signs—rather than the projection of a human presence which the audience assimilates as well as interprets.

13. Not that the question of suicide isn't hovering somewhere in the background. Hamlet's experience has opened a crack in his mind through which despair is always threatening to enter. The Elizabethan audience would recognize familiar arguments for suicide not only here but elsewhere in the play. Cf. Despaire's speech in *The Faerie Queene*, I, ix, which, among other interesting points of comparison to *Hamlet*, uses the figure of the relieved sentinel as an image of easeful death.

## CHAPTER III: OTHELLO'S CAUSE

1. *The Masks of Othello* (University of California Press, 1971), pp. 5, 34, and *passim*.
2. Following F punctuation in l. 325.
3. Following $Q_I$ at l. 86 and again at 91, where the exchange, "I pray . . . handkerchief!" is not in F.These latter lines may represent playhouse interpolation, though the case for Shakespearean authority can be made. Even as an actor's addition, however, they suggest where the theatrical excitement of the scene was felt to lie.
4. Reading "Faith" with $Q_I$ at l. 32.
5. One great distinction of Olivier's Othello was his sensitivity to all these levels of diction.
6. At the end of the speech, Othello's rhetorical failure is even more noticeable. Struggling to construct a coherent image of himself out of contradictory feelings, he arrives at a series of strained and unconvincing formulations, interrupted by gusts of emotion:

> O balmy breath, that dost almost persuade
> Justice to break her sword. One more, one more!
> Be thus when thou art dead, and I will kill thee,
> And love thee after. One more, and that's the last!
> So sweet was ne'er so fatal. I must weep,

But they are cruel tears. This sorrow's heavenly;
It strikes where it doth love.
(V, ii, 16-22)

He is trying for spaciousness and control, but the moral analysis is grotesque, his impulses break apart, he strikes uncomfortable poses.

7. I think that John Bayley is responding, ultimately, to this aspect of Shakespearean tragedy when he says, "With Shakespeare the mere fact and story of consciousness replaces both action and idea. . . . The usurpation by the mind of both practical action and purposeful idea in tragedy—the mind of a murderer, a revenger, a man and woman in love—this is far from being the sum of Shakespearean tragedy; but it is the most important feature of Shakespeare's relations with tragic form" (*Shakespeare and Tragedy* [London, 1981] p. 6). Bayley's book offers a deeply suggestive reading of the tragedies, but I cannot agree with him that consciousness "replaces" action in them. Shakespeare, in my view, sees action as inseparable from consciousness. Mind does not usurp action but interpenetrates with it, and one of Shakespeare's great contributions in tragedy is to make dramatic action out of this relation.

8. I am of course indebted here to Wilson Knight's discussion of *Othello's* imagery, "The Othello Music," *The Wheel of Fire* (London, 1965), pp. 97-119.

9. For the dialectic of "wit and witchcraft" in the play, see Robert Heilman's important *Magic in the Web: Action and Language in Othello* (University of Kentucky Press, 1956).

10. Again, this is not to deny the strong separate interest of Desdemona. Shakespeare, in characteristic fashion, gives her a story and a mind which are in no sense exhausted by the needs of the Othello story. Perhaps most important is the way in which she becomes a center—and ultimately, by her thoughts and actions, a measure—for the competing notions of love which eddy through the drama. In no other

play is Shakespeare more profoundly aware of how the sexual life of women is compromised and shaped by the imaginations of men; Desdemona acts a tragedy of her own in this arena, greater than Hedda Gabler's. But these elaborations, while enriching the play, are outside my subject here. More importantly, as part of the total dramatic experience, they never distract us from our engagement with Othello.

## CHAPTER IV: ACTING AND FEELING: HISTRIONIC IMAGERY IN *KING LEAR*

1. "Histrionic imagery," as I use the term, refers to any element in the text of a play which clearly indicates the manner of an actor's attack, particularly to those which suggest a recurring pattern. The image can be an object or part of the body, as in the examples from *Lear* in the previous section, but, as we are about to see, it can also be a part of speech (Lear's reiterated exclamations), another character (the Fool as Lear addresses him), or even an emotion (Lear's sorrow as he fights to keep it down), anything, in short, which carries with it a specific mechanism or gesture of theatrical self-projection on the part of the actor who engages with it. The lists that Hamlet uses to indicate rapid emotional progressions, the exotic references and locutions that Othello incorporates into his speech, are examples of histrionic imagery. The term is inevitably fuzzy at the edges, because finally everything in a play requires histrionic treatment, and so every object and every word in a dramatic text may be considered a histrionic image. But in practice it is useful to limit the concept to items that can be shown to suggest a reasonably plain and recurrent performance attack.

2. Again, I am using "performance design" in Marvin Rosen-

berg's technical sense—the architecture of histrionic possibilities built into a single role.

3. Note in this passage how "relieve," "pity," and "neighbor," words which carry an opposite sense to monstrosity or violence, take on, by management as well as context, a resistant, snarling texture.

4. Following Dr. Johnson, editors usually gloss "thought-executing" as *acting with the rapidity of thought*. Kenneth Muir also cites Moberly's, "Executing the thought of him who casts you." But there is also a suggestion of capital punishment in "execute," and this sorts well with the aggressive energy of Lear's own thoughts, which will perhaps be punished when his white head is singed. Note that Lear is once more imagining action as proceeding instantaneously and irresistibly from thought.

5. Like any attempt to explain a complex theatrical moment or indeed any complex instant of feeling, this runs the risk of sounding over-intellectualized, but it is in no sense over-elaborate. In a good performance we unmistakably feel both the expansive release of Lear's cry—and the intensity of renewed pain at each iteration. If we don't, we feel the actor is faking: shouting has replaced feeling, generalization experience.

6. This may be heard on Gielgud's *Ages of Man* recording, Columbia OL 5390.

## CHAPTER V: SPEAKING EVIL: LANGUAGE AND ACTION IN *MACBETH*

1. Here are some definitions the *O.E.D.* gives as active at the time *Macbeth* was written: to entreat; to request, petition, or sue; to invite or persuade to some act of lawlessness or insubordination; to allure by specious argument; to court or beg the favor (of a woman), especially with immoral intention; (of things) to affect a person or thing by some

form of physical influence or attraction; to conduct or manage (business affairs, etc.); to conduct (a lawsuit) as a so-
licitor; (of things) to call or ask for, to demand (action,
attention, etc.); to disturb; to make anxious.

2. Following F lineation.

3. Reading "feels" with $Q_2$ (and many editors) at l. 452.

4. *The Political Works of James I*, ed. Charles Howard McIlwain
   (Harvard University Press, 1918), p. 282.

5. For a discussion of the doctrine of equivocation in relation
   to *Macbeth* see Henry N. Paul, *The Royal Play of Macbeth*
   (New York, 1950), pp. 237-47. See also Frank L. Huntley,
   "Macbeth and the Background of Jesuitical Equivocation,"
   *PMLA* 79 (September, 1964), 390-400.

6. *Explorations* (London, 1946), p. 20.

7. Kierkegaard's description of existential choice is very much
   to the point here: "The real action is not the external act,
   but an internal decision in which the individual puts an end
   to mere possibility and identifies himself with the content
   of this thought in order to exist in it. This is the action."
   The dagger speech constitutes an extraordinary analysis of
   this kind of action, the movement of a mind from enter-
   taining a possibility to committing to it. It is at this moment
   in the play—not earlier when the witches tempt him, nor
   later when he strikes the blow—that Macbeth becomes
   Duncan's murderer.

8. Adopting Rowe's widely accepted "tune" for "time" at l.
   235.

9. See Geoffrey Bullough, ed., *Narrative and Dramatic Sources
   of Shakespeare*, VII (London, 1973), 478-79, 481, 482.

10. The sense that Macbeth's criminality is of ambiguous
    origin, that evil comes as if "out of nowhere," is reinforced
    by a general ambiguity about origins in the play. In his
    remarkable study, *"King Lear," "Macbeth," Indefinition,
    and Tragedy* (Yale University Press, 1983), Stephen Booth
    points out that *Macbeth* often leaves us in doubt about
    beginnings, causes, and sources. "In fact, it is almost im-

possible to find the source of any idea in *Macbeth*; every new idea seems already there when it is presented to us. The idea of regicide really originates in the mind of the audience" (p. 94).

## VI. *ANTONY AND CLEOPATRA:* ACTION AS IMAGINATIVE COMMAND

1. The process of transformation is further extended by the play's final procession, which represents a transformation by Cleopatra of the triumph that her Roman conqueror has planned. Regally attired, solemnly and respectfully attended, she is now to be carried, not to humiliation in Rome, but to a famous Egyptian grave, and Caesar himself is glad to claim reflected glory from the spectacle. As an Egyptian procession has brought Cleopatra on-stage at the beginning of the play, a Roman one carries her off, but it, too, celebrates her greatness.

2. Redgrave comments, "You have to create, convincingly, the image of a man who held part of the world in thrall, and you have very little to do it with; all you have is his voluptuousness." (Margaret Lamb, *Antony and Cleopatra on the English Stage* [Associated Universities Press, 1981], p. 147.)

3. An influential and particularly explicit example is John Danby, *Poets on Fortune's Hill* (London, 1952), pp. 128-51.

4. In the role of Cleopatra, Shakespeare makes good use of the boy actor to reinforce this double impression. At the beginning, Cleopatra draws heavily on the boy actor's strong suits of playful bitchery, bright raillery, mockery of the "adult" Roman style, but concludes the play on a sustained level of mature emotion which severely taxes the boy's skills—even while calling attention to his limitations (including, specifically, his whory gestures). Watching the boy Cleopatra, an Elizabethan audience could feel both the theatrical

shallowness of "boying" a woman's greatness and the power of *this* boy to go beyond the normal limits of his art. See *The Actor's Freedom: Toward a Theory of Drama*, pp. 141-45.

5. Following Pope's emendation at l. 38.

## CHAPTER VII:  CHARACTERIZING CORIOLANUS

1. See above, p. 10.
2. For a very persuasive psychoanalytic study of this impression and its source in the play's verbal imagery, see Janet Adelman, " 'Anger's My Meat': Feeding, Dependency, and Aggression in *Coriolanus*," in *Shakespeare: Pattern of Excelling Nature*, ed. David Bevington and Jay L. Halio (University of Delaware Press, 1978), pp. 108-24.
3. "For he was a man to full of passion and choller, and to much given to over selfe will and opinion, as one of a highe minde and great corage, that lacked the gravity, and affabilitie that is gotten with judgment of learning and reason, which only is to be looked for in a governour of state: and that remembred not how wilfulnes is the thing of the world, which a governour of a common wealth for pleasing should shonne, being that which Plato called solitarines. As in the ende, all men that are wilfully geven to a selfe opinion and obstinate minde, and who will never yeld to others reason, but to their owne: remaine without companie, and forsaken of all men."—Geoffrey Bullough, ed., *Narrative and Dramatic Sources of Shakespeare*, V (London, 1964), 519. Plato's term is found in the fourth letter to Dion.

4.                                    Let the Volsces
    Plough Rome, and harrow Italy! I'll never
    Be such a gosling to obey instinct, but stand
    As if a man were author of himself
    And knew no other kin.
                    (V, iii, 33-37)

5. One of the most interesting things about *The Rape of Lucrece* as one of Shakespeare's earliest essays in tragedy is the way it pursues—rather doggedly pursues—the connection Lucrece's act of self-definition makes between contingency and necessity, those hoary topics of tragic theory. Through her long speeches in the center of the poem, Lucrece's tragedy emerges as the story of a woman constrained to act so as to preserve a certain idea of self. Her soliloquy insists on the contingent nature of the rape, on the roles that Opportunity and Time have played in it (ll. 869-1029). Under the stress of events she is forced to act, and each possible action involves a different option for self-definition. If she wishes to be the ideal Roman wife, she must kill herself. Once she has made that choice she has no choice, but the choice characterizes her for all time. Responding to the horrors of contingency, she puts on necessity. And Tarquin, whether he likes it or not, has chosen too. But each act produces further contingencies, which in turn demand new puttings-on of necessity by the heroic self. At the end of the poem, Lucrece plus time plus opportunity provides the formula for Brutus' self-defining decision to intervene (1807-48). He takes advantage of the general horror at Lucrece's suicide to abandon his masquerade as a simpleton and lead a successful rebellion against the Tarquins. His political act, in turn, becomes an event of radical importance to succeeding generations. Later, at another crucial moment in history, as Shakespeare and his readers were well aware, Junius Brutus would himself become a rallying cry. Something of the haunting tragic connection between necessity and contingency may be felt when Lucrece addresses time as "Thou ceaseless lackey to eternity" (967).

# Index

## Library of Congress Cataloging in Publication Data

Goldman, Michael, 1936-
    Acting and action in Shakespearean tragedy.

    Bibliography: p.
    Includes index.
    1. Shakespeare, William, 1564-1616—Tragedies.
2. Shakespeare, William, 1564-1616—Dramatic production.
I. Title.
PR2983.G64 1985    822.3'3    84-17745
ISBN 0-691-06630-2 (alk. paper)